Chronicle Your Life with Drawing, Painting, Le

THE ART OF THE

travel journal

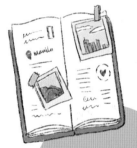

Document Your
Adventures,
Wherever They
Take You

Abbey Sy

QUARRY

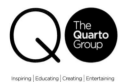

Inspiring | Educating | Creating | Entertaining

Brimming with creative inspiration, how-to projects, and useful information to enrich your everyday life, quarto.com is a favorite destination for those pursuing their interests and passions.

© 2022 Quarto Publishing Group USA Inc.
Text and images © 2022 Abigail Sy

First Published in 2022 by Quarry Books, an imprint of The Quarto Group,
100 Cummings Center, Suite 265-D, Beverly, MA 01915, USA.
T (978) 282-9590 F (978) 283-2742 Quarto.com

Quarry Books titles are also available at discount for retail, wholesale, promotional, and bulk purchase. For details, contact the Special Sales Manager by email at specialsales@quarto.com or by mail at The Quarto Group, Attn: Special Sales Manager, 100 Cummings Center, Suite 265-D, Beverly, MA 01915, USA.

10   9   8   7   6   5   4   3   2

ISBN: 978-0-7603-7621-8

Digital edition published in 2022
eISBN: 978-0-7603-7622-5

Library of Congress Cataloging-in-Publication Data is available.

Design: Megan Jones Design
Cover Image: Cherisse Elaine Y. Yao
Page Layout: Megan Jones Design
Photography: Cherisse Elaine Y. Yao
Illustration: Abbey Sy

Printed in Singapore

This book is dedicated to the artist and adventurer in all of us. May you enjoy the journey and make wonderful memories from your travels.

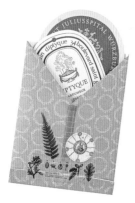

CONTENTS

1

Getting Started ...8

2

Materials ...22

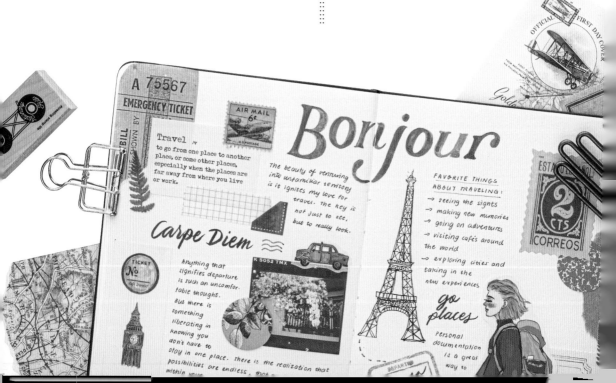

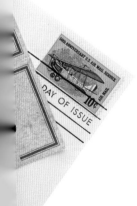

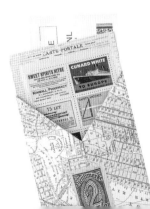

Introduction

How I Started Travel Journaling

I've been documenting and journaling about my life since I was thirteen, but it wasn't until I was twenty years old that I accidentally discovered travel journaling.

The first time I kept a travel journal was during my first trip to Europe in 2013. I was in Paris, waiting in line outside the Louvre in the cold, and I had nothing else to do. I remember having a small journal with me and a fineliner pen, so I created drawings about my trip for a half hour while the line was moving.

The idea of keeping a journal while traveling was not something I knew of back then, mostly because the concept of travel was foreign to me at a young age. I didn't know that it was possible to go from one place to another by way of airplanes, ships, and trains. As someone who grew up mostly glued to studying, my fascination for travel came later in life and coincided with my love for documenting, which subsequently opened a new avenue for my creative expression.

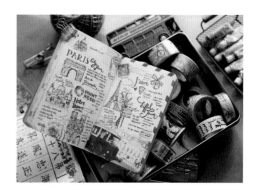

As the years went on, my love for documenting unfolded in different ways. I traveled a lot; as a self-employed artist and author, journaling was my main escape. In one journal, I would sketch architecture from Budapest. In another, I would stick all the packaging and tickets I got from a day trip to Kyoto. Eventually, I kept more and more journals, and I've discovered that this medium has allowed me to creatively explore and experiment in the best way I can.

Many of my journal pages are a collection of experiences and memories that linger in my mind. My travels over the years signify specific periods in my life that are full of learning and exploration as I try to build a connection with cities I encounter from every part of the world.

How to Use This Book

Hey there, fellow artist!

I'm so glad you picked up this book, and I hope you'll find it useful for your creative endeavors.

The Art of the Travel Journal, in essence, is a compendium of ideas and inspiration you can use as you start or continue your travel journaling pursuits.

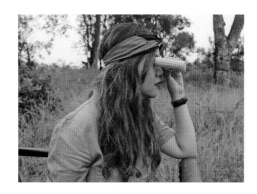

Keeping a journal is a great way to be in tune with your memories and experiences in the years to come, whether you're looking for a way to document your day-to-day life or explore new cities.

Here are some ways you can maximize the use of this book:

- **Set an intention.** Why do you want to keep a travel journal? Identifying this early on helps give you ideas for how you want to document your adventures.

- **Define your journaling style or preferences.** What topics interest you while traveling, and which ones do you want to document?

- **Choose the tools that you need to create.** In this book, I share different art tools, journal types, and writing materials you can try for journaling. This will help you decide which supplies you want to use for a specific trip, depending on your chosen art medium.

- **Get inspiration from the journal spreads.** I've been keeping travel journals for many years now, and I hope you find inspiration from the spreads I've made. I've enjoyed the process of experimenting with the craft, such as creating sketches and ephemera-filled journal pages, and I hope you do, too.

- **Try your hand at different styles.** You'll find a handful of tutorials inside this book to guide you, including how to hand letter a full page and create collages. These lessons allow you to explore a variety of ways you can document your travels.

Remember, the best part of where you're going is where you are right now. That holds true, too, as you pick up your journal and start writing about your own travel stories and adventures. I'm looking forward to seeing what you create and document as you embark on your journey.

Always Be Creating,

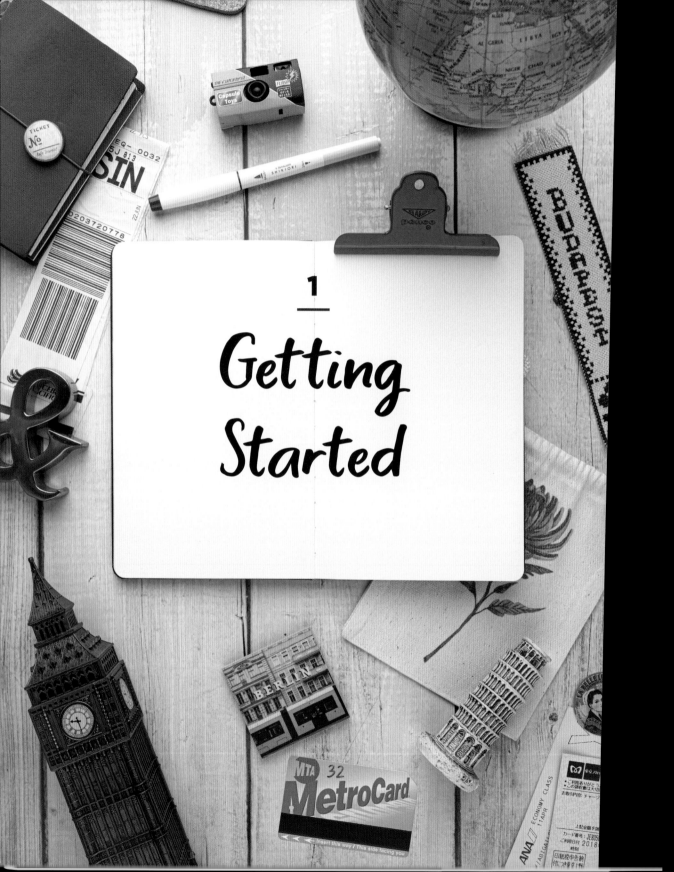

1

Getting
Started

Ready to embark on this new journey? This chapter is all about how travel and journaling started, what you need to start your own travel journal, and some great reasons why you should document your travels and adventures.

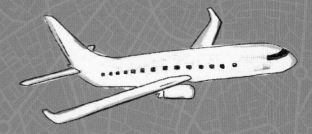

DEFINITION OF JOURNALING TERMS

Becoming familiar with these terms will help you better understand the process of journaling and what it entails. Feel free to refer to it anytime you need a refresher.

Analog: Not involving or relating to the use of computer technology, in contrast to a digital counterpart

Archive: A collection of historical documents or records providing information about a place, institution, or group of people

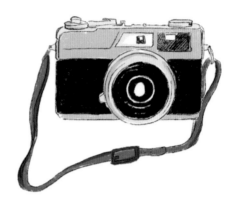

Collage: A piece of art made by attaching a variety of materials, such as photographs, paper, or fabric, onto a backing

Diary: A consistent personal record of thoughts, reflections, and experiences

Ephemera: Collectible memorabilia, usually made of paper, such as postcards, posters, maps, and tickets, that were intended to last a short time when they were produced

Hand lettering: The art of creating lettering by hand in any font style

Journal: A personal record of thoughts, reflections, and experiences

Journaling: To keep a journal; to enter or record thoughts and experiences

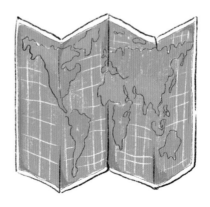

Plein air: The activity of painting outdoors, derived from nineteenth-century French Impressionism

Transit: The act of passing through or across a place

Travel: To go on a trip or journey

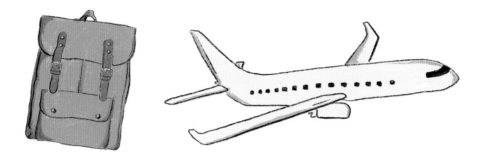

Travel guides: A type of publication with practical information and tips or advice about a certain destination, meant for people who want to visit that place

Travel journal: A place for writing about and documenting trips, including what was learned and experienced

Travel stories: A type of travel writing featuring a narrative about a journey, usually meant for literary purposes

Travelogue: A type of travel writing in the form of a journal or itinerary style featuring places visited and explorations experienced by a traveler, usually written in the first person and told in the past tense

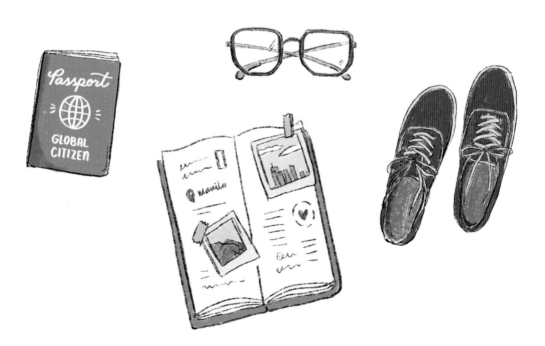

A BRIEF HISTORY OF TRAVEL JOURNALING

Ancient Travel

Traveling for pleasure in ancient times started in Greece, when Greeks would visit sporting events such as the Olympics or make a trip to Egypt to see the extraordinary Pyramids of Giza.

In the sixth century, Japanese travelers began making special trips to Japanese spas, also called *onsen*, which are still a go-to place for Japanese travelers and tourists alike. For Muslims, making a pilgrimage to Mecca originated during the same time period.

The Grand Tour

European nobility visited cities such as Rome, Paris, and Seville in the seventeenth and eighteenth centuries and would write about their journeys in the form of poetry, songs, or literary pieces. This was called the Grand Tour, and it was an educational rite of passage for the nobility as they came of age. This tour typically lasted months or years, and these young adults were accompanied by a knowledgeable guide or tutor throughout the journey.

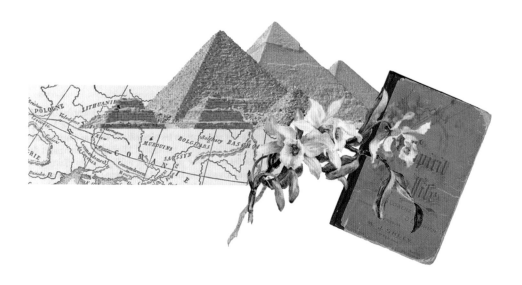

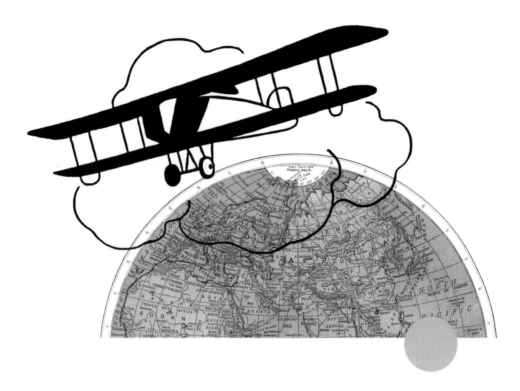

Modern Travel

The world's first commercial airplane, the St. Petersburg–Tampa Airboat Line, flew across Tampa Bay, Florida, in 1914. This was a short-lived precedent to modern air travel, but it paved the way for regular transcontinental flights in the years that followed.

In recent years, travel has no longer become a luxury but a commodity. Around the world, travelers are taking a detour from their daily lives or finding an escape from reality for a week or a few months. Travel has become a universal activity and provides a way for us to keep exploring and discovering what is out there.

WRITING ABOUT TRAVEL

The idea of writing about travel originated hundreds of years ago, albeit in different forms. In medieval times, some works were a combination of fact and fiction for literary purposes, revealing that people didn't know much about the world around them. Some pieces were glamorized for literary purposes.

Here are some notable writers who were able to capture travel in their work:

- The *Odyssey* by Homer recounted Odysseus's long journey home after the Trojan War. This epic is regarded as one of the most significant works of the Western canon, with themes centered on the ideas of wandering, return, guest-friendship, and omens.

- *Anabasis*, or *The March Up Country*, by ancient Greek professional soldier and writer Xenophon, narrates the expedition of a Persian prince against his brother, King Artaxerxes II, as well as the Greek troops' travels through Asia back home to Greece.

- In China, Xu Xiake's travel records and diaries contained accurate details of specific measurements and information of his geographical discoveries with over 404,000 written Chinese characters. Most of these travel records were topographical and paved the way for discovering factual accounts of land and sea that were not recognized at the time.

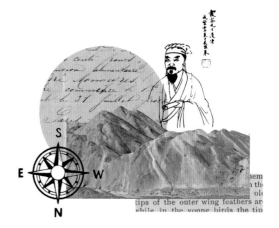

- *Il Milione*, or *The Travels of Marco Polo*, is a travelogue written by Rustichello da Pisa in the thirteenth century, based on stories told by Marco Polo from his travels and experiences through Asia between 1271 and 1295.

JOURNALING

By the late eighteenth century, explorers such as Captain Cook, Lewis and Clark, and Charles Darwin recorded their observations and findings about the world through their journals. Keeping journals proved to be a record of information that would serve as the foundation for human progression and discovery, with topics ranging from explorations of the Pacific Ocean to the origin of species.

The art of journaling became a staple for writers, artists, and other creatives. This was an integral part of the creative process as it became a valuable way of documenting their lives and work. Some of the most prominent artists and writers who kept diaries include Leo Tolstoy, Franz Kafka, Virginia Woolf, Katherine Mansfield, Anaïs Nin, and Sylvia Plath.

The rise of war journals in the nineteenth and twentieth centuries offered a written account of people's experiences. The act of chronicling and reporting events, such as Anne Frank's diary and war soldiers' chronicles, became prominent features of the times.

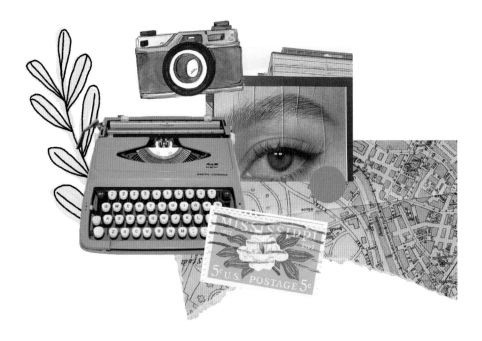

As the digital age emerged, journaling through blogging became a medium that many people discovered was worth exploring. In 1993 and 1994, author Jeff Greenwald pioneered the first international blog as he circled the globe and posted real-time dispatches to Global Network Navigator (GNN), the first commercial web publication at that time.

Fast-forward to the 2010s, when travel blogging became a lifestyle and a job for some. Writing about tourism and cultures has opened numerous possibilities for digital nomads to explore and earn a living at the same time.

In recent years, putting pen to paper has become prevalent again, especially with the rise of interest in stationery, traveling, and journals. There's something so personal about writing, documenting, and creating pages in a journal that makes it such a coveted activity. Many people are finding that travel journaling is an avenue for self-discovery and instrumental for improving mental health.

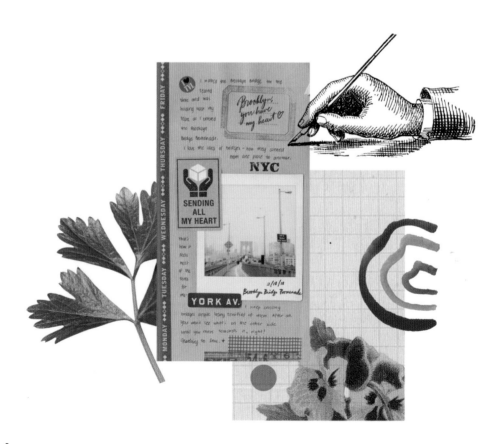

STARTING A TRAVEL JOURNAL

Starting a travel journal can be overwhelming at first. With so many options, ideas, and ways to document, it's no surprise that many people are intimidated by this journaling format. But beginning a journal isn't difficult if you take some factors into consideration. Here are some ideas for how to start a travel journal.

Find Your "Why"

Why do you want to start a travel journal?

For most of us, it's about having a record of experiences to look back on and serve as a memory-keeping tool. But journals can also be an avenue for creative expression, a personal project, or a new hobby. If you're searching for a way to appreciate travel on a deeper level, travel journaling can be a catalyst for that.

Once you find your reason for travel journaling, the rest becomes easier. You're able to serve your main purpose of starting a travel journal, and you'll understand the fundamental purpose of your documenting journey.

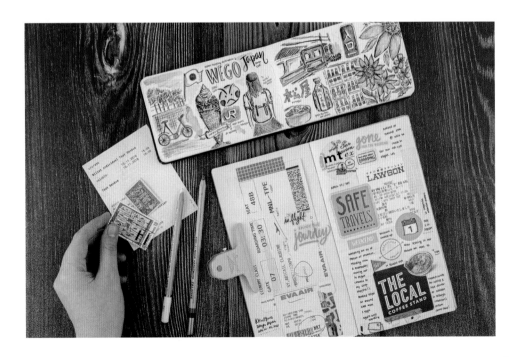

Identify Your Travel Goals

Not all trips are the same, and there's no right way to experience a trip. But it's important to know what you want to document about your travels and whether those elements are aligned with your goals.

An example of a travel goal is exploring different parts of a country or a city, such as Berlin or New York, or trying out cafés in Italy, or going on hiking adventures or beach trips. Consider how and why you travel as your basis for setting goals. Setting goals enables you to discover what you want while choosing what to document.

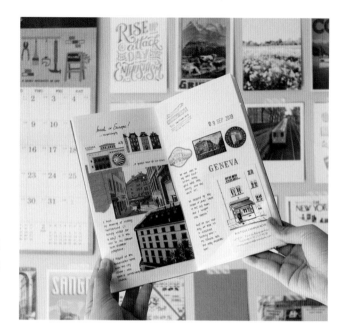

Choose Your Creative Outlet

Do you like to write about your day-to-day happenings when traveling? Perhaps you're the type who instantly picks up your smartphone and snaps a photo or collects tickets, maps, and brochures from museums and theme parks. Maybe you capture the essence of a city by sketching it.

Knowing what you like to do—or want to try—while traveling helps establish the creative outlets you can use to document your travels. You can choose one or many.

Research Ideas

Look for journal spreads or ideas online or in magazines or books that resonate with how you want your pages to look. These can be color scheme ideas or anything that helps you visualize the creative approach you'd like to take. While these inspirations may embody your ideal journal, don't rely too much on them as a basis for your documenting process—trust your own instincts and creativity.

THE BENEFITS OF KEEPING A TRAVEL JOURNAL

Creating a travel journal offers much more than a physical reminder of your travels. These benefits are worth considering.

Creates Something to Look Forward To

Keeping a travel journal helps build anticipation even before you start to travel, whether it's planning your trip, daydreaming about your future adventures, or creating a bucket list of sights to see. You can also start gathering information and thinking about what's to come as you make plans and decide where to go.

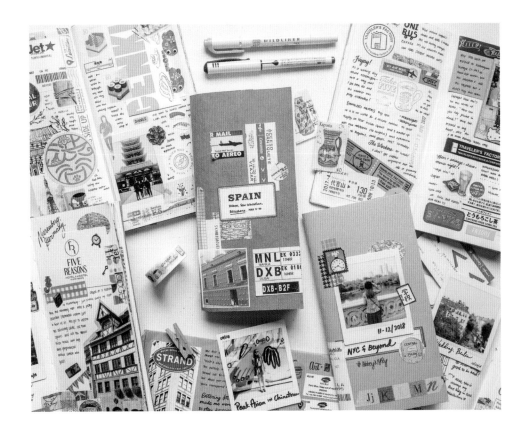

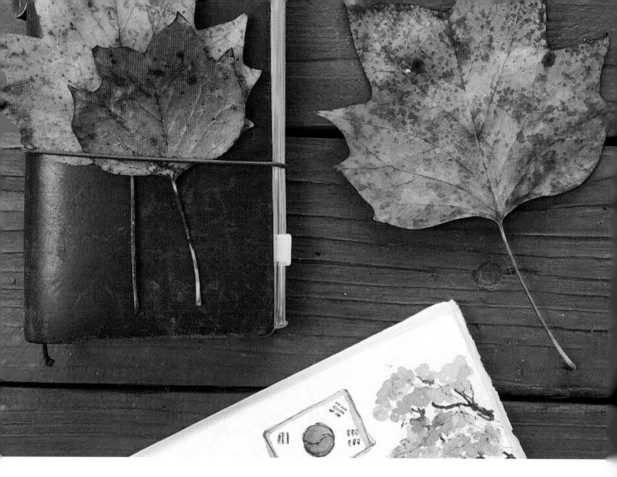

Develops Your Creative Vision

One of the best things about traveling is being creatively inspired by a foreign place. Keeping a travel journal allows you to preserve key moments on paper and at the same time capture moments as they happen. Travel journaling encompasses a variety of styles, so you're able to develop your creative vision as you continue exploring and experimenting.

Cultivates Curiosity and Fuels Discovery

Asking questions drives curiosity and in turn helps us discover more about the world around us. When traveling, there's so much to unravel in every place you encounter, such as cultures, food, geography, architecture, and the people you meet. Having a place to record these experiences makes the process enriching and provides a memorable way to revisit your travels.

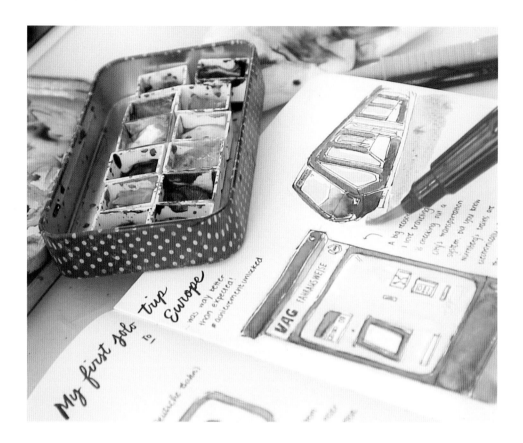

Provides a Creative Outlet

Keeping a travel journal encourages creativity. That shift to the creative right side of the brain inspires you to think of ways to be creative and document your trip using familiar techniques and tools you have with you. Writing in your travel journal also allows you to organize your thoughts and creates richer memories that will forever be documented in the pages of your journal.

Promotes Mindfulness and Reflection

Every trip you embark on and how you see, hear, touch, taste, and smell while traveling is unique to you. This helps promote mindfulness as well; we're reminded to be here now, in this moment, and savor it. Travel journaling lets you remember and reflect on those moments. What did you enjoy about the trip? What were your thoughts about it? How did the trip make you feel?

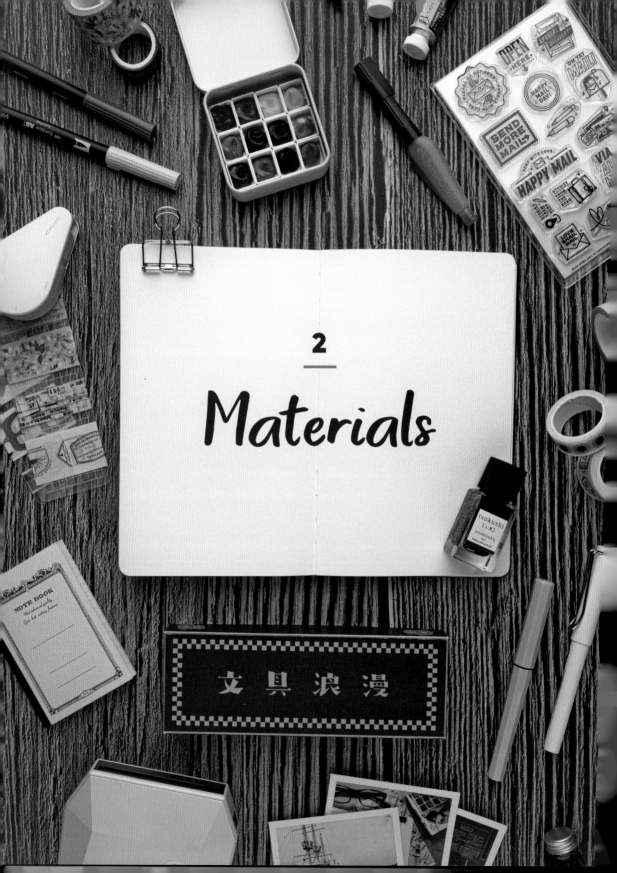

2
Materials

Now that you know the basics, it's time to familiarize yourself with the tools and materials you can use to create your travel journal pages. This chapter highlights the key supplies to add to your arsenal of travel journaling essentials, such as pens, paint, paper, craft tools, and various size journals.

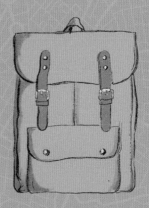

ESSENTIAL SUPPLIES

Choosing the best art supplies for creating journals can be daunting, whether you have no materials or hundreds of options. The pens, paints, brushes, journals, and other items included here are ones I've used to chronicle my travels. I encourage you to experiment with supplies and see which ones may become your favorites.

Notebooks

One of the first decisions you'll make as you start documenting your adventures is choosing a notebook to serve as your travel journal. Since this will be your blank canvas, it's important to choose a size, paper type, and style that work for you so you can use the journal to its full potential.

These are the most common sizes of travel journals.

- **A5 journal:** 5.86" × 8.25" (15 × 21 cm). This is an ideal size for all creative practices, such as drawing or painting, writing, and photography.
- **Slim journal:** 4.75" × 8.75" (12.1 × 22.2 cm). The slim journal is a common size for collage-style journaling due to its slender format.
- **A6 journal:** 4.1" × 5.8" (10 × 15 cm). This size is easily portable and great for making notes or doing pocket journaling.

A6 JOURNAL

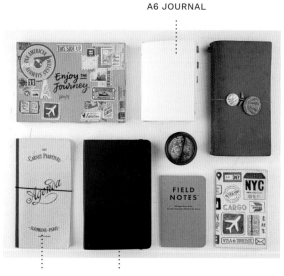

SLIM JOURNAL   A5 JOURNAL

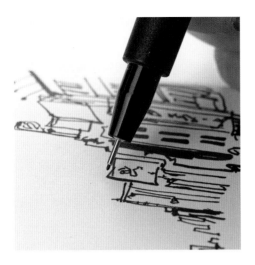

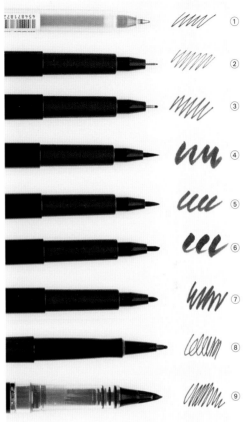

Pens

FINELINER PEN

This is my pick for the best pen for drawing and sketching. Fineliners come in a wide range of nib sizes (from 0.005 mm to 1 mm) and colors (black, neutrals such as brown and gray, and every color of the rainbow). These pens are usually waterproof and are preferred by most journaling enthusiasts for their durability and efficiency.

BRUSH PEN

This pen typically has a nib that mimics a paintbrush and is great for lettering and shading. Some are water-soluble, making them a hybrid of watercolors and brushes and a nice alternative to watercolor paint.

① GEL PEN
② FINELINER PEN (0.2 MM)
③ FINELINER PEN (0.5 MM)
④ BRUSH PEN (SOFT TIP)
⑤ BRUSH PEN (HARD TIP)
⑥ BRUSH PEN (SOFT CHISEL TIP)
⑦ FELT-TIP PEN (0.8 MM)
⑧ FELT-TIP PEN (0.5 MM)
⑨ FELT-TIP PEN (0.3 MM)

GEL PEN

These pens use pigments suspended in a water-based gel and are used mostly for writing and illustration. They're easy to find in office supply and general merchandise stores and are widely used in schools and offices. They come in different colors and nib sizes and write smoothly on paper. Most gel pens come in sets of colors and styles to suit each person's needs.

FOUNTAIN PEN

A fountain pen has a metal nib that applies water-based or waterproof ink to paper. This is a level up from gel pens, for good reason: Its refillable mechanism makes it economical and convenient. For writing and sketching, a fountain pen is more ergonomic because it requires less pressure from your hand than a regular pen.

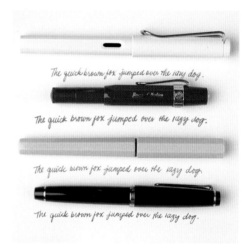

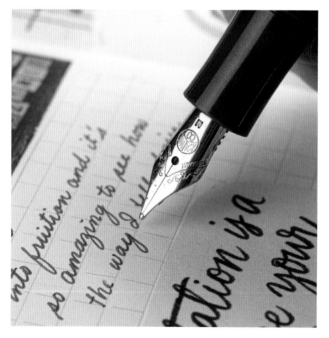

While they are more expensive than regular office pens, fountain pens can last for years in your pen collection if well cared for, and they make great travel companions. The range of nib sizes and designs suits every person's preference and lifestyle.

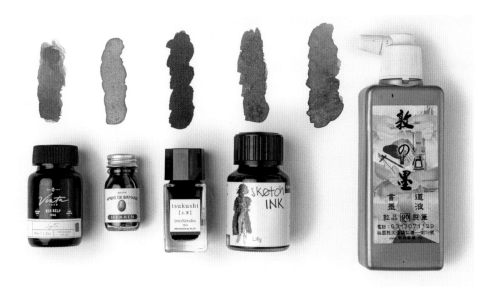

FOUNTAIN PEN INKS

Inks have different properties and come in an array of colors. They also behave differently on different types of paper, so it's important to know the types of travel journals and papers you'll be using and which ink colors you prefer.

Most fountain pen inks are water-based, meaning they are not waterproof and are recommended for writing or quick sketches. If you're using fountain pens with watercolor paint or other mediums, waterproof fountain pen ink is recommended.

Pencils, Brushes, and Paint

PENCILS

Drawing pencils are arranged by grade; some have harder or softer leads, producing lighter or darker lines. A hard lead pencil (grade H) produces lighter strokes and is recommended for creating illustrations. These come in several types, but 2H or 3H pencils are safe choices.

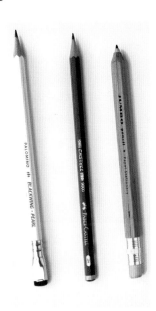

PAINTBRUSHES

Brushes come in a variety of sizes and bristle types, including synthetic and natural. Using paintbrushes with paints and inks allows you to add color and texture to your artwork. I recommend using synthetic brushes for lettering, and large and small natural brushes for painting background subjects and details, respectively. My favorite is a round size 4 synthetic brush as it works for both lettering and painting.

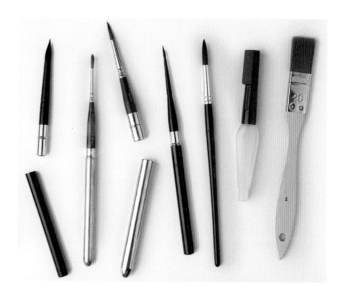

WATER BRUSHES

Water brushes feature a compartment that can be filled with water, making them the most versatile paintbrushes for travel journaling because you don't need a separate water container. Simply squeeze the body to force water into the brush, where it mixes with paint for convenient watercolor painting.

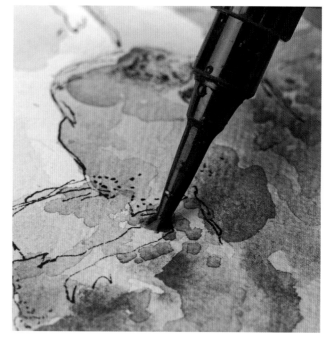

WATERCOLORS

Watercolors are transparent in nature and are great for painting travel-themed subjects, making them a top choice for travel journaling.

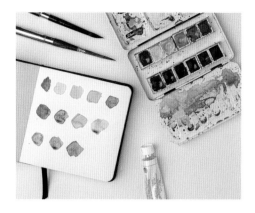

Many artists choose watercolors for journaling because they're a versatile medium. Their transparency makes it easy to build layers of color, and they're available in different forms.

- **Pans:** Dry watercolor pigment is set into small pans and arranged in a palette. This is the ideal option for painting on the go, but the paint needs to be rehydrated with water before using.
- **Tubes:** Pigment mixed with a binder is packed in tubes, and the paint can be used as is or diluted with water.

GOUACHE

Gouache paint is a water-based paint that's more opaque than watercolor and great for layering. Its higher pigment load ensures more saturated color. Gouache is a good option if you like painting scenes or bold patterns and letters in your travel journals.

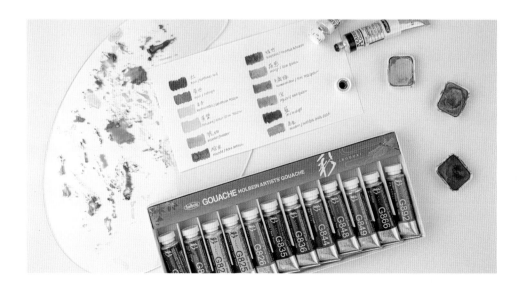

Paper

WATERCOLOR PAPER

This paper is primarily used for watercolor painting because it holds paint well and resists wrinkling. For thickness, use at least 200gsm and above (this is the weight of the paper and will be listed on the package) to make sure water doesn't seep through the paper.

Watercolor paper can be made of cellulose, which is recommended for practice work, or cotton, which is more expensive but best for archival work.

You can buy watercolor paper in a pad, where the pages are bound together in notebook form, or in a block, where individual pages are glued together on the sides and can be detached.

Hot press paper has a smooth texture and cold press paper has a rough texture.

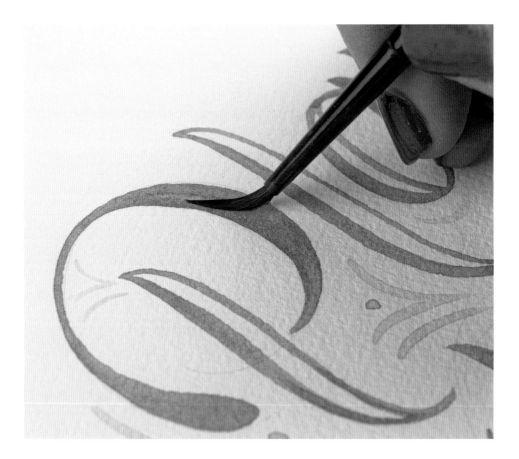

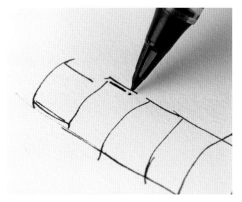

SKETCH PAPER

SKETCH PAPER

Sketch paper is good for sketches and drawings; the paper should have a thickness of at least 80gsm so ink doesn't bleed through.

FOUNTAIN PEN–FRIENDLY PAPER

This type of paper is compatible with fountain pens; it's generally smooth, and ink won't feather.

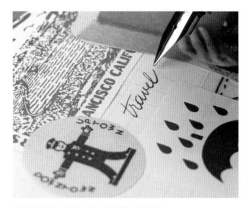

FOUNTAIN PEN–FRIENDLY PAPER

KRAFT PAPER

Kraft paper is ideal for collage (see page 61) and junk journaling due to its durable paper weight; 70gsm to 100gsm weight is ideal.

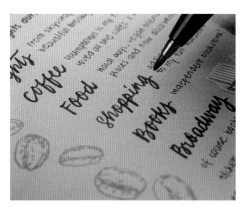

KRAFT PAPER

LINED PAPER:
for longform
writing

PLAIN PAPER:
for sketching
or painting

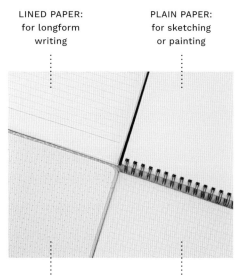

DOTTED PAPER:
for collage, writing,
or sketching

GRID PAPER:
for collage, writing,
or sketching

CUTTER　　WASHI TAPE　　BONE FOLDER　　STICKERS

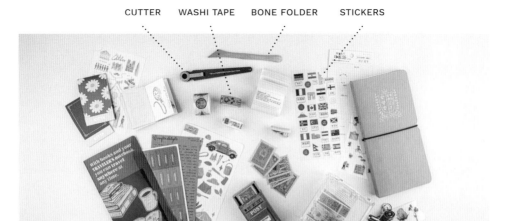

WASHI TAPE: decorative and functional lightweight tapes for journaling
STICKERS: used for decorating and collaging in journals
BONE FOLDER: a tool for scoring and folding cards and pieces of paper (these are typically
　　made out of cow bone but can also be found in plastic, wood, and Teflon)
CUTTER: for cutting and shaping specific elements or paper

STAMPS　　　　　　　CLEAR BLOCK　　GLUE TAPE

STAMP PAD INK

SCISSORS

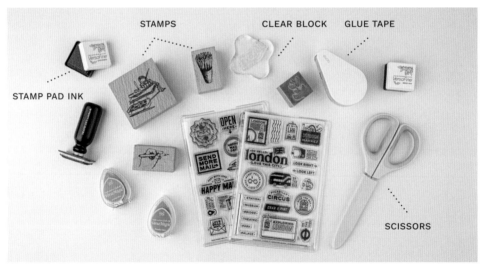

STAMPS: to decorate and enhance journal pages (these include clear, wood-mount,
　　and cling-mount stamps)
STAMP PAD INK: used for stamping on journal pages. Ink comes in a variety of types,
　　such as archival (which is usually waterproof), pigment, and hybrid. Archival ink,
　　which resists fading, is best for travel journaling.
CLEAR BLOCK: used to temporarily mount clear stamps for stamping
SCISSORS: for cutting and crafting
GLUE TAPE: adhesive for sticking photos or paper

OTHER TOOLS

These optional supplies are great supplementary tools that will add interest to your journal pages.

Typewriter

A typewriter is a nice addition to your travel journaling tools collection, whether it's a secondhand purchase from a flea market or a brand-new machine. There's something so nostalgic about using a typewriter to type paragraphs of text or just phrases to decorate your travel journals.

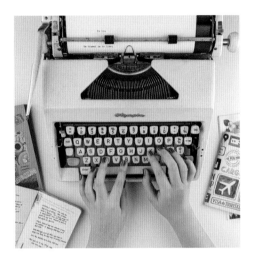

Printer

Several types of printers are available, including traditional tabletop ones, instant photo printers, thermal printers, and portable pocket printers. Portable printers, some no larger than a cell phone, enable you to print photos on the go.

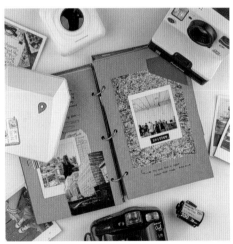

Camera

A camera is an invaluable tool for documenting snippets of your travels, whether it's an instant camera, film or digital camera, or your smartphone. Photos provide references that can be used for drawing or journaling about your trip.

CREATING A TRAVEL ART KIT

Creating a travel art kit is an effective way to assemble your documenting essentials on the go. This is one example of what a travel art kit could contain. You can add or edit these materials, depending on your preferred mediums.

- **Pocket notebook:** for keeping records, quick notes, or random ideas
- **Larger journal:** main documenting supply
- **Pocket watercolor tin:** for painting on the go
- **Water brush:** no need for a separate water container because water is contained in the barrel of the brush
- **Pens:** for writing notes, sketching, and doodling
- **Envelopes (commercial or handmade, see page 55):** for storing ephemera and other small items
- **Glue:** for adhering ephemera (glue sticks work great for traveling)
- **Pocket scissors:** handy tool for trimming ephemera or packaging to include in your journal
- **Decorative tapes:** for embellishing journal spreads
- **Pouch:** for storing all your essentials (extra points if it has a lot of pockets)

Space is always at a premium when traveling. Making your own storage pieces lets you pack supplies efficiently and tailor your materials to your needs.

Lesson

CREATE YOUR OWN WASHI TAPE SAMPLER

Stocking bulky rolls of washi tape in your travel art kit isn't the most ideal setup if you want to travel light. Carry your favorite tapes while in transit by making low-profile tape samplers.

MATERIALS

· 3 to 5 washi tape rolls

· Plastic washi card (also called PVC card; these are available online) or old gift card

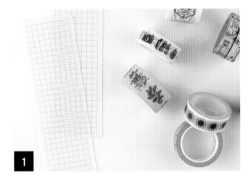

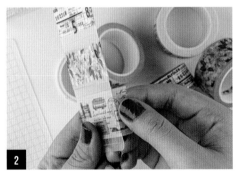

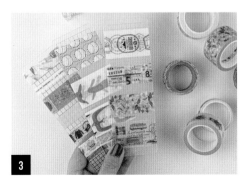

1   Choose tape colors and patterns you want to travel with that fit on the plastic card. Usually, three to five tapes can fit on one card, depending on the tape widths (some measure between 1 and 2 cm). Choose tapes that fit your themes or color palettes.

2   Start at the top of the card and wrap the first roll five to ten times around, depending on how much you need. Continue to wrap the tapes, leaving a space between each roll. Continue this process until you reach the end of the card.

3   Make as many washi tape cards as space will allow.

MAKE YOUR OWN WATERCOLOR TIN

Filling a small tin box with a custom watercolor palette averts the hassle of bringing a full watercolor set. Here's how to make your own watercolor tin to add to your travel kit.

1   Gather all your materials. Place the pans in the tin to determine how many it can hold. You'll need at least four to six colors.

2   Choose the watercolor paint tubes for your kit. I recommend selecting a variety of warm and cool colors, but this can vary depending on the subjects you'll be painting, such as landscapes, people, or objects.

3   Place adhesive on the bottoms of the watercolor pans and position the pans inside the tin. The more snug the pans, the less they'll move.

MATERIALS

·   Half pans (these are small square plastic cups that hold tube watercolors and measure 0.6" × 0.7" [15 × 19 mm] and 0.4" [10 mm] deep; they typically hold 0.3 to 0.4 teaspoons [1.5 to 2 ml]) or full pans (about 0.8" × 1.2" [20 × 30 mm] and 0.4" [10 mm] deep; they typically hold 0.6 to 0.7 teaspoons [2.8 to 3.5 ml])

·   Compact tin or box (recycled mint containers work well)

·   Tube (liquid) watercolors in your preferred colors

·   Adhesive (strong double-sided tape, Blu Tack reusable adhesive, or magnet strips)

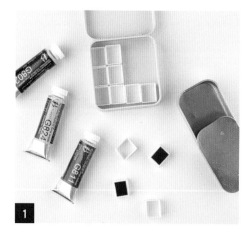

1

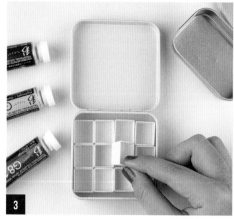

3

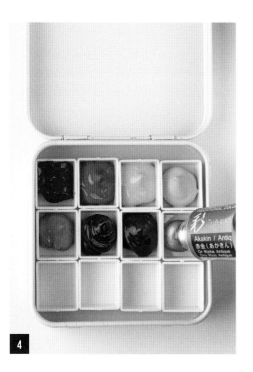

4 Gently squeeze each color inside its corresponding pan. Fill each pan to 75 percent capacity to avoid spillage.

5 Once all the colors have been added, allow the paint to dry for at least 24 hours. The paints should be completely dry before you travel.

6 Swatch the colors in your travel journal for a handy visual reference. This watercolor kit is meant to be used with a water brush (see page 28) for a more convenient travel journaling experience.

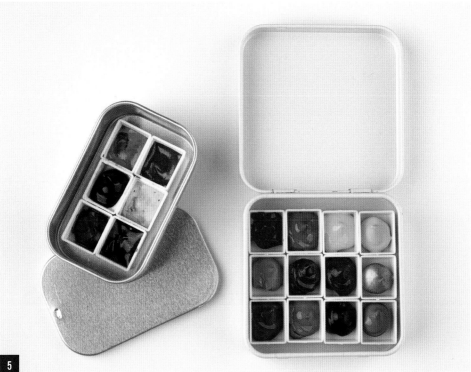

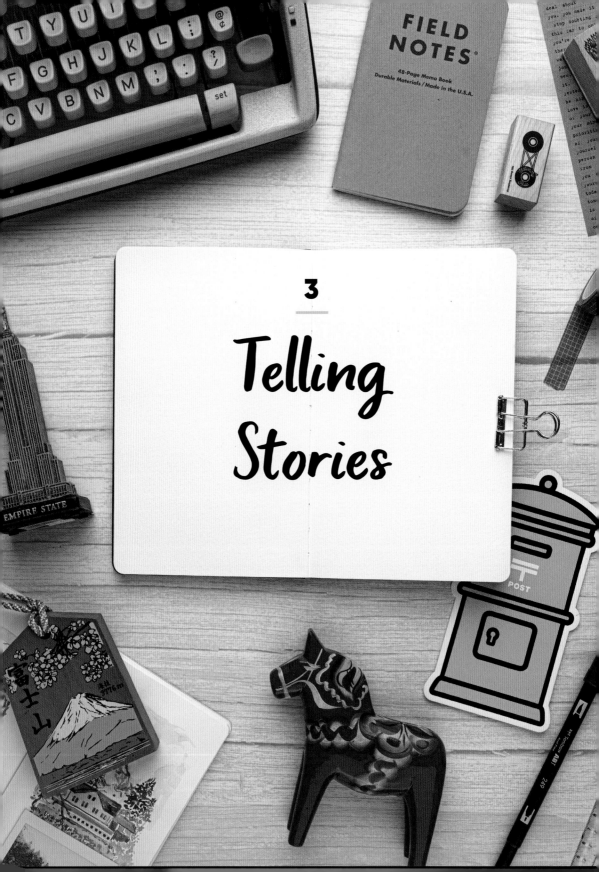

3

Telling Stories

Whether you're traveling for the first time or are a seasoned tourist, this chapter offers ideas to inspire your trips, including planning your itinerary and documenting in transit. You'll also find tips and ideas on how you can creatively document your travels, depending on your goals and destination.

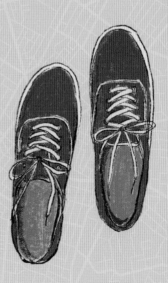

PRE-TRIP PLANNING

Once you've planned and laid the groundwork for your trip, it's time to strategize the trip itself. Here are things to consider while preparing for your upcoming trip.

Establish Your Trip Goals

Are you traveling for work, leisure, or both? Visiting a place for the first time? Seeing a specific exhibition, or trying the local fare? Determining your goals for a trip is key for narrowing down what to include in your itinerary.

Consider Your Interests

Make a list of your favorite activities and interests, such as art, books, coffee and cafés, food, shopping, or visiting tourist spots. Reconnect them with your goals. Do they match?

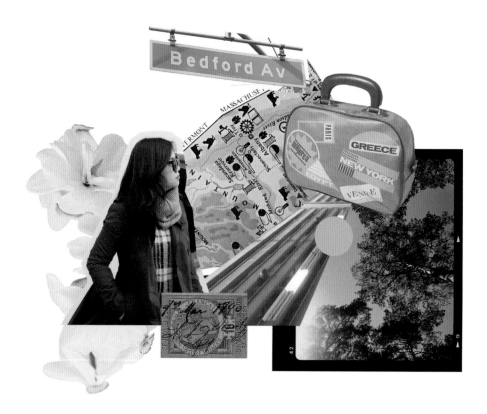

Calculate Your Budget

A trip budget can range from backpack friendly to peak expensive, so take this into consideration. Having a budget in mind before you take off can help you determine when you can splurge and when you should save. Venice, Italy, for example, is filled with beautiful stationery stores stocked with expensive leather journals and beautifully decorated papers; if those are on your must-have list, make sure you've got the funds.

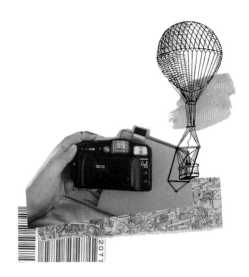

Research Your Destination

Get to know the cities and towns you're planning to visit. Learn what they're known for, what the weather will be like when you visit, and the ideal accommodations that fit your budget. Find out whether you need to book tickets in advance for museums or events—this is especially important during summer and major holidays, which are peak travel times. Then, see how the results of your research align with your goals, interests, and budget.

Plot and Schedule

Here comes the fun part: planning it all out. Make sure that your schedules are editable to enable flexibility. Unforeseen events, such as weather conditions or establishments being closed, can cause disruptions, so have alternative plans or ideas in place.

WAYS TO DOCUMENT YOUR TRAVELS

Documenting my travels is an essential part of my adventures. Every time I see something that piques my interest, I document it.

I don't like sticking to one style of documenting. On some trips, I draw all the buildings and structures, and on others I simply print photos and add ephemera to my journal along with some writing. When traveling to places I've been several times, I fill pages of notebooks with my thoughts and musings. My creative preferences vary because each place inspires me to be creative in different ways.

I bring at least a notebook on all of my trips, and I play around with my creative juices. Explore a variety of ways to document your travels using both analog and digital formats.

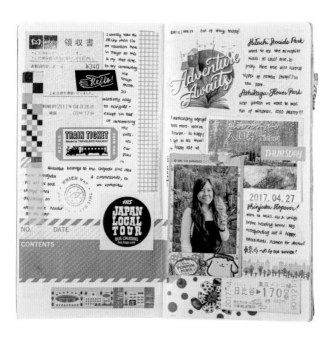

Analog

COLLAGE JOURNALING

The art of putting papers, photos, and other memorabilia together to create a collage is an easy and creative way to get started with documenting your travels. If you love keeping ephemera from every trip, collage-style journaling is a great fit. I'll share more tips and ideas on collage-style journaling in the next chapter.

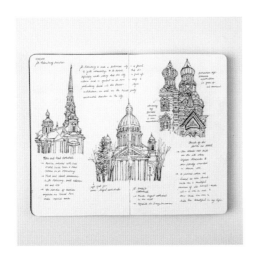

ILLUSTRATED JOURNAL

Illustrating what you see or experience in a city is another way to record your trip. I particularly enjoy this format when I'm visiting a place for the first time and I study the architecture and discover more of the surroundings. Drawing gives me a chance to view things from my own perspective, and you'll experience that too.

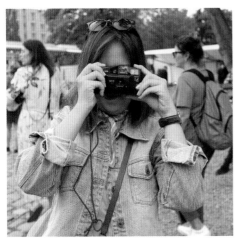

FILM PHOTOGRAPHY

Capturing photos on film is different from snapping away on your smartphone. There's something special about taking photos on a film camera, because you won't see the images until the film roll gets developed. The photos themselves can be appealingly grainy (depending on the film and camera) and full of character, making this a fun activity to try.

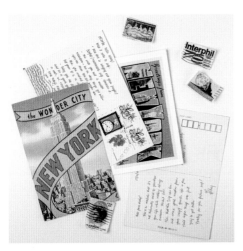

POSTCARDS

The art of correspondence is such a beautiful reminder of the passage of time. When I lived abroad, I sent myself a postcard every week to share stories my future self could read. This is a personal and meaningful way to remember your trips, from choosing a postcard design and postage stamps to sending the card in the mail.

Digital

PHOTO BOOK

A photo book contains mostly photographs (and sometimes text) taken during a trip and is custom-created using digital software. I enjoy collating photos and documenting my trips through photo books because they're tangible and a nice addition to my travel memorabilia. If you love taking photos, making photo books may be right up your alley.

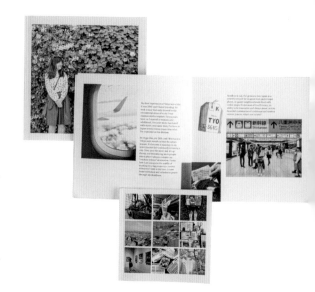

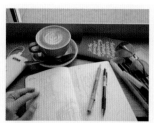

Coffee & Food
Coffee in New York
Favorite cafes from the Big Apple.

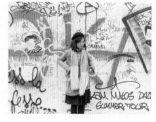

Europe
Cold Days and Colder Nights
A month of quiet time in Berlin.

BLOG POSTS

Blogging captures a snapshot of moments and emotions expressed in words and allows you to narrate a trip or share snippets of places you want to highlight. Writing blog posts has always been a fundamental way for me to document—I started blogging about my trips with the main purpose of sharing recommendations and experiences. But blogging can also be a personal endeavor and an exercise in creative writing that's worth exploring.

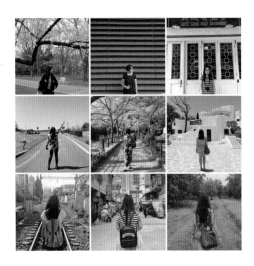

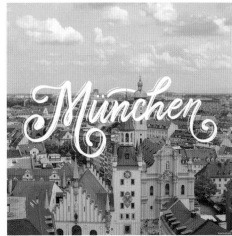

VISUAL DIARY

Keeping a visual diary of your travels through photos (which you can add to your photo books, too) helps create a graphic memory of your adventures. You can create a series of photos that have a similar theme or style, or you can give them a specific Instagram hashtag (I tag my travel photos with the hashtag #ABCEnRoute on Instagram). As much as this is a visual treat for anyone who sees it, I use it as a personal record of my travels.

I like to make artwork out of my photos, so I letter the locations on the actual photos, and I pose with my back turned in different locations. This is my way of compiling my travel photos into one series.

VLOGS

I've been dabbling with filming lately, and this has made me appreciate travel even more, especially because it is a moving medium. Vloggers capture what they see in unique ways, and this distinctive point of view excites me

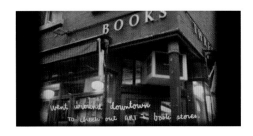

about vlogging. Sharing a variety of experiences, offbeat places, and the mundanity of travel (not everything has to be eventful) is a nice way to experiment and explore outside of photography.

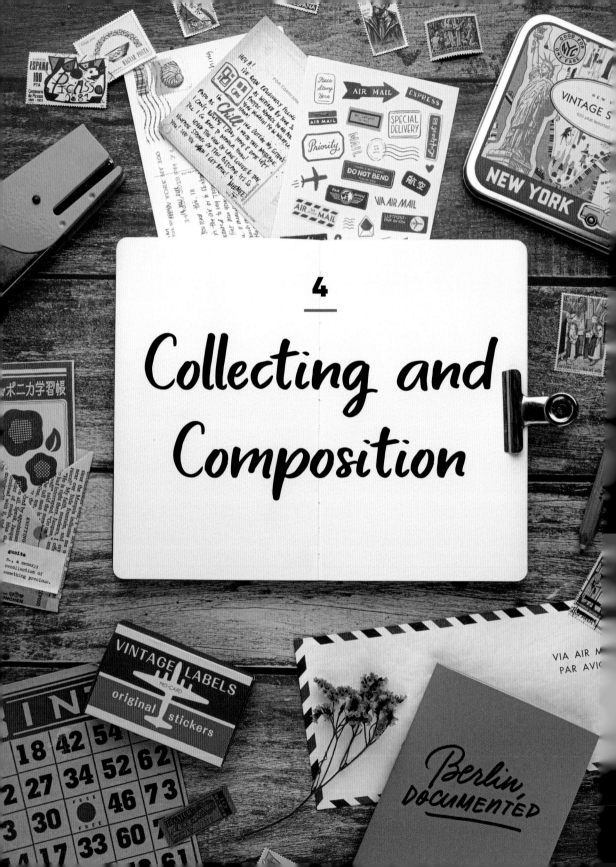

4

Collecting and Composition

This chapter is all about collecting (tickets, maps, brochures, photos, packaging, menus, etc.) and composition (how to put those fun pieces together to make a cohesive journal page or spread). Learn more about the art of collage and create your own layouts to make your travel memories last.

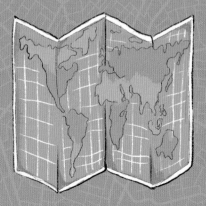

EPHEMERA

Ephemera is any form of printed matter produced for a specific short-term use. The word *ephemera* comes from the Greek word *ephemeros*, meaning "short-lived."

Collecting ephemera such as tickets, maps, and brochures has become incredibly popular, and not just for journaling—sometimes just as a hobby itself. The ephemeral state of memorabilia that has served its short-lived purpose makes it charming and unique.

Ephemera from different parts of the world are all varying in terms of design and size, and it's interesting to see how these mundane items contribute so much to our visual understanding of places we're traveling to.

My first encounter with ephemera was on a two-week trip to Japan in the spring of 2016. While visiting different museums and taking train rides to and from different parts of Tokyo, I realized I'd been unconsciously keeping pieces of paper— mostly because they were too precious to throw away!—as evidence of my trips: maps, train tickets, brochures, and more. I never threw them away, and they're still stored in my analog archive of travel memorabilia.

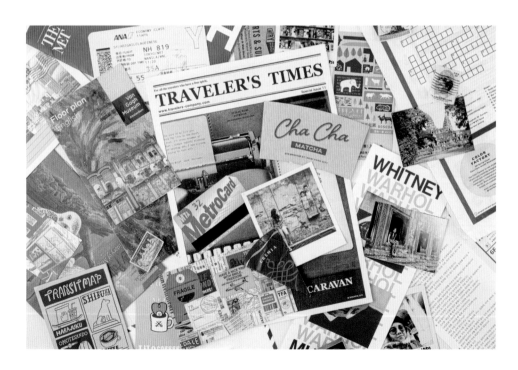

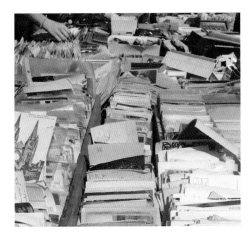
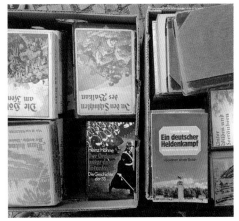

TREASURES AT THE MAUERPARK FLEA MARKET IN BERLIN, GERMANY

As the years went on and I visited new cities, I built a habit of collecting ephemera wherever I went. I also frequented places like flea markets (Mauerpark in Berlin is my favorite) to check out vintage ephemera that I could collect and use for my next creative project. Looking for these items and giving them a new life is always so inspiring.

I carefully hand-select each piece that goes into my ephemera collection, whether it's an old clothing tag, a beautifully designed label on a tin can, or a used coffee sleeve. All are reminders of a certain place in time; some I paste into my collage journal, and others are kept safely tucked away. Many hidden treasures can be found in offbeat places, such as a pub or an underground gallery, and it's often a surprise when you encounter them and can add them to your growing ephemera collection.

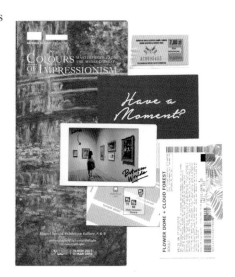

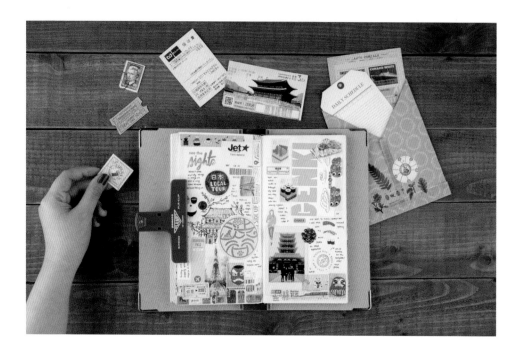

Types of Ephemera (and Where to Find Them)

Ephemera is available in many different forms that you can collect and buy. Your goal as a traveler is to be observant and find these pieces in unexpected spots. I love collecting these types of ephemera, and I hope you will discover some favorites too.

MAPS

Maps are the first things I look for when I'm in a new location such as an airport, amusement park, city, or museum. They're usually given free to provide easier navigation for visitors, and they make for great collectible ephemera. Maps are also good to have on hand if you plan to revisit a location in the future.

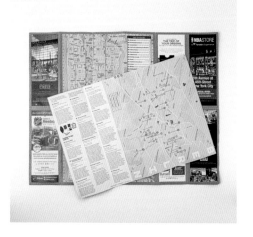

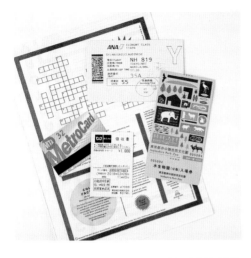

TICKETS

These come in the form of boarding passes, train stubs, concert tickets, and the like. Be sure to keep an eye out for their expiration date—don't turn tickets into ephemera yet if they're good for a few days or weeks (especially train tickets). These days, most tickets are issued digitally, but when you chance upon a ticketing machine, take it as an opportunity to collect printed tickets whenever it's possible.

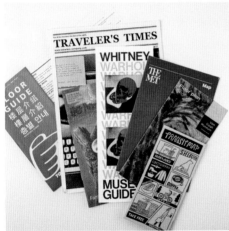

BROCHURES

Free brochures are usually available at retail or specialty stores. These are great to keep and use for journaling, especially if you'll be documenting the store you visited.

PACKAGING

Sometimes I can't bear to throw out beautiful packaging—even ice cream cone wrappers and coffee sleeves. You can find these at supermarkets, convenience stores, souvenir shops, or even on the street if there's an outdoor food market. Make sure to keep packaging dry; if it's greasy or has food residue, throw it out.

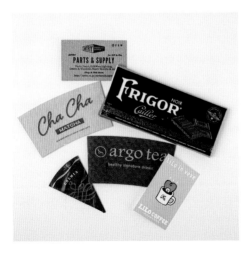

POSTAGE STAMPS

I love collecting vintage postage stamps, and you can often find them in sets at flea markets. I'm intrigued by the different locations and designs featured in each set. Vintage postage is also great to use as extra decoration for written correspondence.

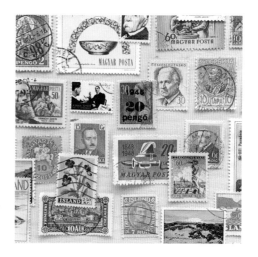

POSTCARDS

A postcard is the most inexpensive souvenir you can find. Depending on the design, these cards can double as ephemera and an art print. Every country and city has its own versions, and the range of designs and styles is amazing. My collection includes more than a hundred postcards, which are a mix of ones from friends and ones I've sent to myself.

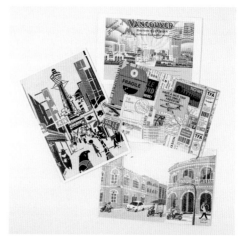

PHOTOGRAPHS

Photographs are among the most personal ephemera you can collect, whether you're using an instant camera, shooting film, or developing photos for analog documenting. In addition to your own photos, you can find vintage photos (some dating back all the way to the nineteenth century) in flea markets or specialty stores, which you can use for collages.

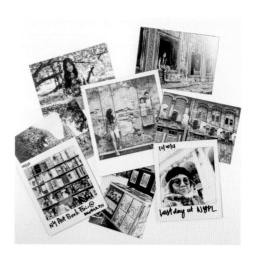

STAYING ORGANIZED

When I collect a handful of ephemera, the first thing I do (especially if I'm on a long trip) is organize the pieces however I see fit: by color, location, or size. I usually carry an ephemera envelope or pocket zip folder for organizing everything. Sometimes I'll find storage supplies at a dollar store while traveling.

Sorting through ephemera when you get home can be overwhelming, so doing it while traveling is a great way to organize a collection, especially when memories are fresh and you're familiar with the activities that happened each day.

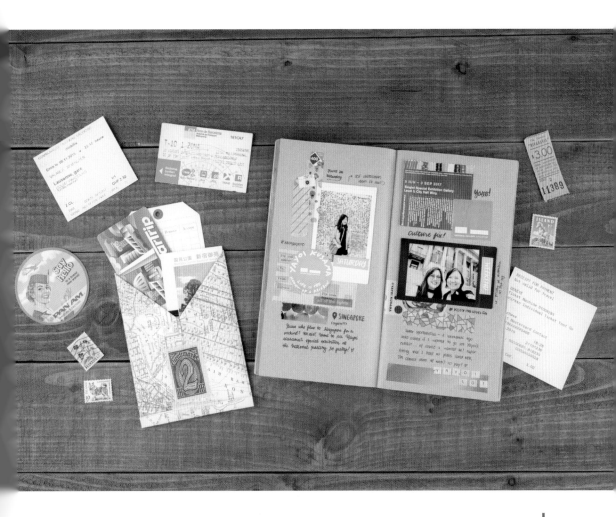

Collect and Select

Every bit of ephemera won't be used for journaling, and that's fine. I try to get multiples of things so I can keep one piece and use one piece, but choosing which ones you'll add to your journal is important. You can also opt to use everything for journaling—it's up to you.

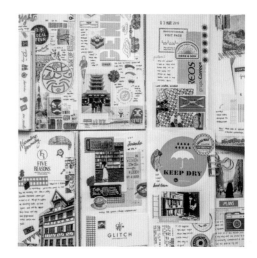

Adding every single ticket or map to your journal pages is tempting, but before you do, take a few things into consideration. If a folded map is especially thick, for example, you may have to cut it up and use key parts for your journal. Some types of ephemera might not adhere with glue, and certain kinds of food packaging aren't suitable for journaling. Ultimately, resourcefulness is crucial when using ephemera for journaling.

Make It Your Own

One of the nice things about journaling with ephemera is its uniqueness—you won't find the same pages elsewhere, and that makes each page your own. While creating pages and spreads, pay attention to your preferences when it comes to journaling and adding elements.

Are you the type who likes covering every page, or do you like to keep some white space showing? Perhaps you tend to choose warm colors as a foundation for journaling with ephemera (like me!)? Making a design your own allows you to unleash your creativity while further developing your journaling style.

MAKING EPHEMERA ENVELOPES AND POCKETS

Lesson

Storing loose papers or ephemera you've collected into handmade envelopes or pockets is an easy way to file them as you travel, before incorporating them into your journal pages. The attractive envelopes also add a fun, decorative element to your journal pages. The best part about these envelopes is that you don't need new paper or cardstock. Try using travel itineraries, maps, or brochures.

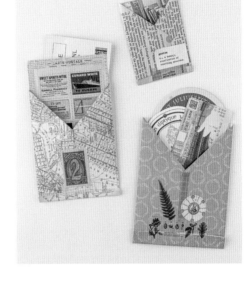

MATERIALS
....

- A5 or A6 size paper (white, kraft, or recycled)

- Stickers or decorative tape, such as washi tape

- Scissors

1   Fold the sheet of paper in half widthwise (**A**). Unfold it, then fold each side into the middle fold, resulting in four even segments (**B**).

(continued)

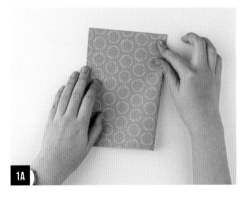

1A

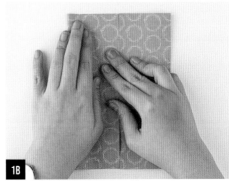

1B

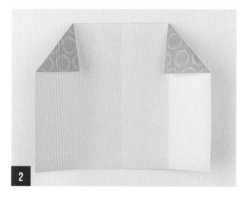
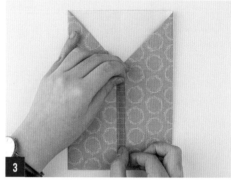
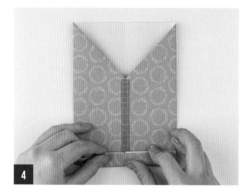
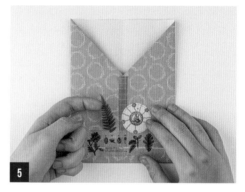

2   Fold in both top outer edges to the nearest fold, creating two triangles at the top left and right sides of the paper.

3   Fold each side toward the middle and seal the center seam with decorative tape, cutting the tape to size.

4   Fold the bottom up about ½" (1.3 cm) to create a pocket and secure it with decorative tape.

5   Decorate the pocket envelope using stamps, stickers, or tapes.

CREATING ARTFUL POSTCARDS

Sending postcards to friends or loved ones is one way to share your adventures with others—or even to your future self, if you send one to yourself (see page 43). This lesson shows you how to make your own postcards and offers ideas for what to write to make them truly personal and unique.

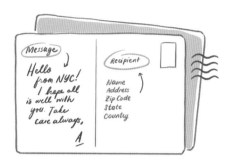

The size of a basic postcard is about 3½" × 5" (9 × 12.7 cm) with 0.007" (0.02 cm) in thickness. I use or 4" × 6" (10 × 15 cm).

If a postcard lacks a template for the name and address, draw it yourself or use a rubber stamp that has this template. Try this easy watercolor lettering technique by making a hand-lettered postcard with a favorite quote.

(continued)

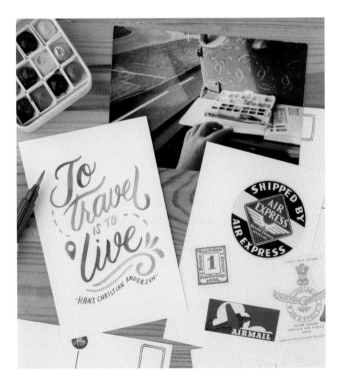

MATERIALS

....

- Cardstock
- Pencil
- Watercolors
- Water brush

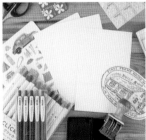

Things to Remember When Sending Postcards

·::

- There should be a recipient name and address, complete with zip code and country.

- Your name and address don't need to be on the postcard, but it's a good idea to include it if the recipient's address is wrong or unreadable or the postcard is undeliverable.

- Postage fees for postcards vary per city and country, so research the cost beforehand and also make sure your addresses are up-to-date.

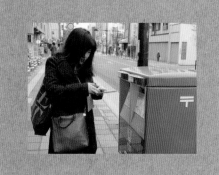

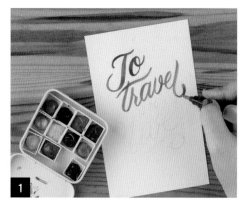

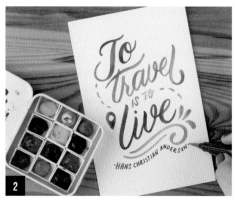

1 On cardstock, outline the letters and other elements with pencil. I chose a simple script font and short quote to fit my card. Fill in the lettering with watercolor paint, using the water brush.

2 Add embellishments to the lettering, such as dotted lines, swirls, and swooshes, and a geolocation marker. Use a variety of colors from your palette. Add the quote attribution in watercolor using a different font. Let the paint dry thoroughly. Your postcard is now ready to be written and sent.

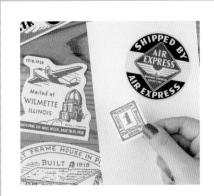

Got some spare stickers in your stationery stash? Use them as a simple design element for a postcard.

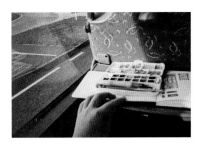

If you love taking photos, consider using some as your postcard design. Simply write your message on the opposite side of the card and you're good to go.

Things to Remember When Making Your Own Postcards

- Make sure the design doesn't include any offensive motifs or words because it will be seen by officials and may get flagged.
- Keep the artwork and designs flat. Dimensional elements might get destroyed in transit, and that isn't ideal. If you would like to add three-dimensional pieces to your cards, consider sending them in an envelope instead of as a regular postcard.
- Use durable, heavyweight cardstock to ensure that it stays in one piece when it's received. Acceptable paper weights are 100gsm to 300gsm (see more on paper weight on page 30).

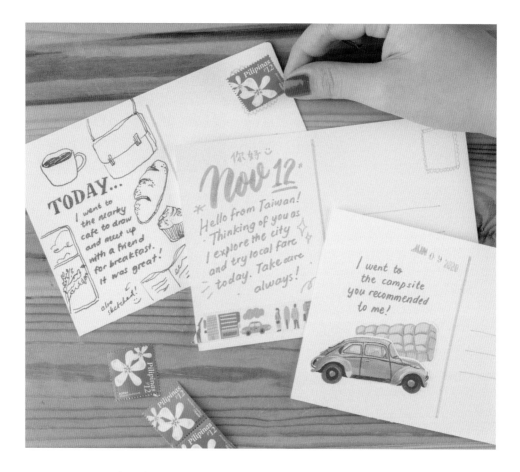

Message Inspiration

Looking for ideas for what to write on your postcards? Here are some you can try:

- A new word or phrase you learned in a foreign language
- A doodle of your travels and trip highlights
- What you did that day, a short anecdote, or a list of activities

Things to remember when writing your postcard message:

- Avoid writing confidential information as it can be accessed by the public.
- Keep your message short and sweet. Think about capturing a moment in time in your postcard.
- Allot space between your message and the recipient's address. This makes it easier to identify the information.

COLLAGE TIPS AND IDEAS

A collage is an art technique that involves combining various materials such as photographs, pieces of fabric, paper, and other ephemera on a surface. In travel journaling, it's referred to as collage journaling.

Before we go any further, let's get this out of the way: there is no right or wrong way to collage. The simple act of cutting and pasting is the only thing you need to know to start.

Digital and traditional collage require cutting and pasting as part of the process. The factors to consider are what to cut, where to paste, and how to put these elements together. With collage, precision doesn't define whether a piece works or not. If anything, my perfectionism seemed to vanish the moment I decided to collage on canvas. It's up to you to create whatever you want to convey through this unique genre.

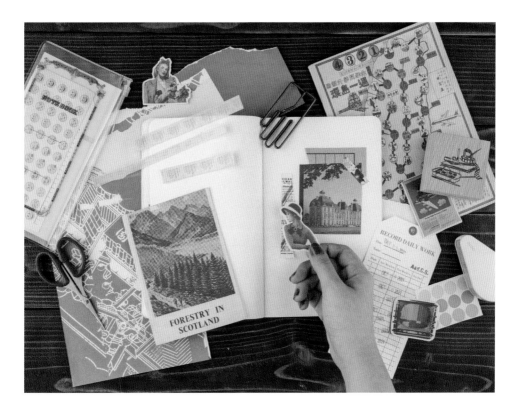

When I started collaging, I came from a background of doing things very specifically, and I developed a very perfectionist attitude when it came to making art. Trying out collage helped me break out of my shell and explore different things as well as embrace happy accidents that happen on a canvas. It not only helped me understand my creative process even more, but it also inspired me to explore ways I can break free from reaching perfection.

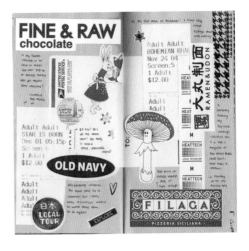

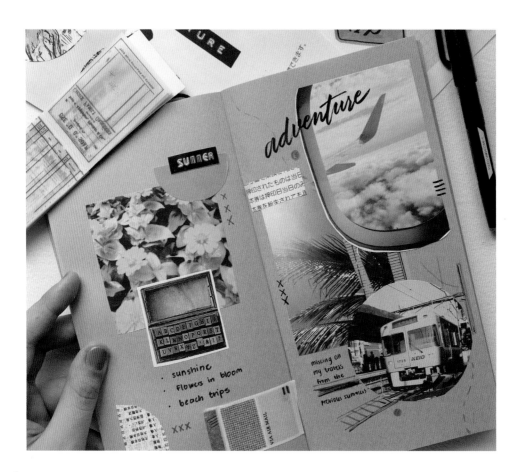

Creating Compositions

Although collage entails adhering materials to a surface, a piece will feel more cohesive if you compose it well. Composition is key when it comes to creating collage. These key factors contribute to the success of a piece.

- A composition based on color: analogous or complementary.
- A composition based on shape: add a multitude of shapes and textures to create depth.
- A composition based on size: scale certain elements up or down to create different illusions from your collage.

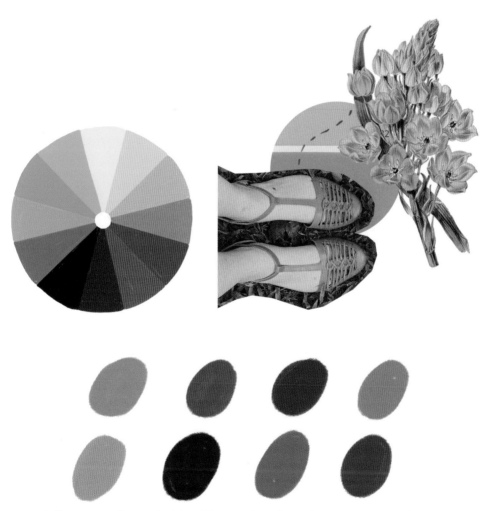

Challenge yourself to work with a different color palette when creating a journal spread.

Choosing a Focal Point

I try to start my collages with a focal point or key message, although this isn't always a rule. The focal point can be a dominant color or subject, and I work my way from there. Typically I choose a large piece, such as a photo or big cutout. Trust your instincts for whatever catches your eye and use that to guide your work.

Establishing a focal point also helps establish the direction of your layout. You get to decide where a person looks or where you can lead them in your artwork.

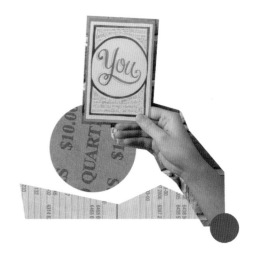

Exploring and Experimenting

My favorite way to collage is to always experiment with something new, whether it's a new shape, a new color scheme, or new elements that I can layer on top of each other. A little bit of resourcefulness and creativity can go a long way when it comes to creating a collage.

A tip I live by is to work with what you have. If you have an envelope full of random plane tickets or a collection of stamps and maps waiting to be used, now is the time to explore different ways to document your adventures using what you have. I hope you find collaging to be a fun activity to incorporate into your travel journaling, whether it's a small part of a journal page or pages that become a full canvas.

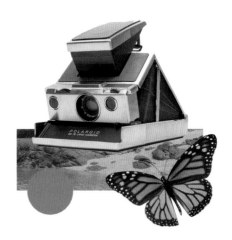

Lesson | MAKE A COLLAGE TRAVEL ZINE

A zine is a self-published work, usually produced in limited numbers, that incorporates original artwork and/or ephemera and text. Making a travel zine to capture important moments of your trip is another creative way to document your adventures. Creating a zine is also a great way to warm up and practice techniques such as collage as you produce more travel journal spreads about your trip. Working with an A4-size sheet of paper provides countless possibilities to make art, write, or do collage. Anything goes!

MATERIALS

- A4 paper (8.5" × 11" paper may be substituted)
- Stationery supplies, such as washi tape, stickers, stamps, and ephemera
- Scissors
- Adhesive
- Gel pens or other favorite pens

(continued)

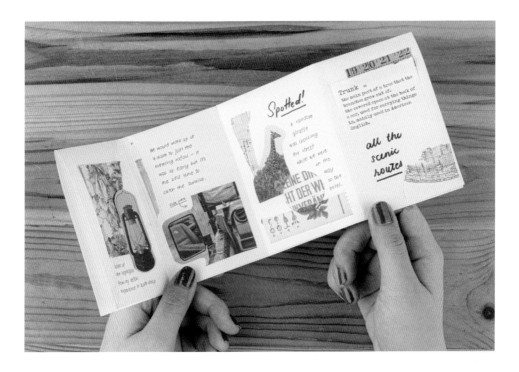

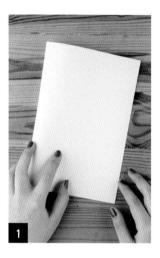
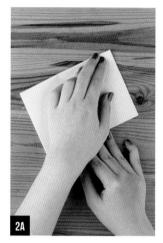
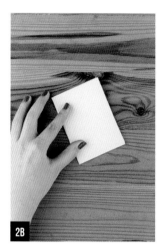

1   Begin by creating a series of folds that will become the pages of the zine. Fold the sheet of paper in half widthwise.

2   Fold it in half again widthwise (A). Fold the sheet in half lengthwise (B).

3   Unfold the sheet and you should have eight same-size rectangles. These will be your zine pages.

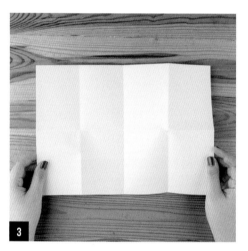

4   Use this diagram to mark the pages; when the zine is folded into its pocket size, the pages will be sequential as numbered. The orientation of each page will be portrait, so it's best to take note of that while designing. The last two boxes on the bottom right serve as the front and back covers, and the remaining boxes make up the content (see photo with step 9 for the correct page orientation).

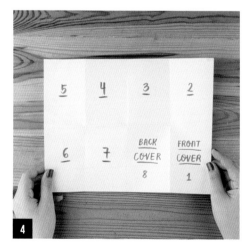

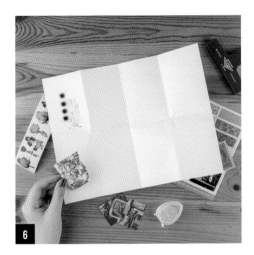

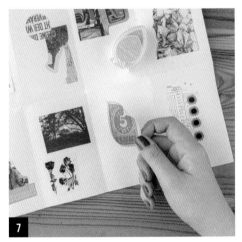

5   Once the pages have been marked, it's time to think about what your zine will be about. Some ideas to consider:

- List style: five to ten highlights or favorites from your trip
- Food you've tried
- Tourist attractions you've visited
- A daily log of events (for a week or less)
- Doodles or drawings captured over several days

6   Now comes the fun part: designing your zine pages. I'll walk you through my entire zine design process. Your zine will be unique, but I hope this offers some guidance when creating your own. I usually start with decorating each page with stickers and tape. This helps me establish the overall aesthetic of the zine, and I don't feel overwhelmed.

7   This zine is about my trip to South Africa, so I chose safari-inspired colors such as yellows, greens, and browns for my stationery and ephemera (see more about working with color palettes on page 99).

(continued)

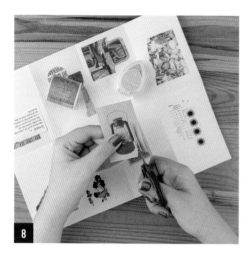

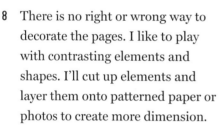

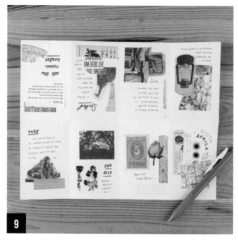

8   There is no right or wrong way to decorate the pages. I like to play with contrasting elements and shapes. I'll cut up elements and layer them onto patterned paper or photos to create more dimension.

When it comes to collaging on a small canvas, I try to place elements first on each page and see if the positioning works. This helps develop your composition skills, especially when you're working with different types of paper.

I also consider how the text and other components factor in as I finalize my pieces. After repositioning them and seeing which ones work best, I'll eventually make a decision based on my observations and adhere them.

9   Journal on the pages if you like; I use a gel pen. I try to round up the whole zine through journaling, so I keep my text to a minimum and usually add captions to some pages that feature photos.

Here are some questions I asked myself while working on the zine:

- What stood out to me while going on a safari for the first time?
- What was our trip schedule like?
- How was the overall trip?

It helps to have an overarching theme to tie your story together. I chose key points that were distinct and memorable to me as a traveler.

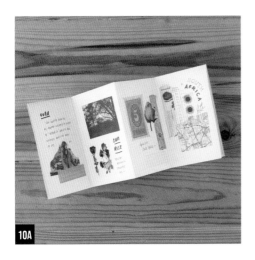

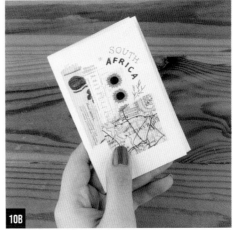

10A **10B**

10 Once I'm happy with the pages and covers, I fold it back and it's done (**10A**). Repeat the original folding sequence (see page 66) to close the zine (**10B**):

- Fold the paper in half widthwise.
- Fold it in half again widthwise.
- Fold the sheet in half lengthwise.

You can incorporate zines into your travel journals or store them in a designated folder, envelope, or storage box for safekeeping. Take them out when you want to relive some of your favorite moments or simply browse and share with family and loved ones.

Tips for Making Your Own Travel Zine

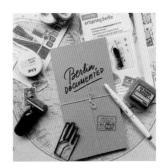

These ideas will come in handy when making a zine about your trips.

- Don't overthink it! The best part of a zine is that the pages are small, and a few elements are all that's needed to complete a page. This allows you to expand your ideas on the rest of the zine pages.
- Make and make and make. The more you do, the more you'll enjoy the process.
- Add variety. Zines don't have to stick to one theme. You can make a series of zines from one trip, dividing them into different themes. Get creative and your ideas will flow.

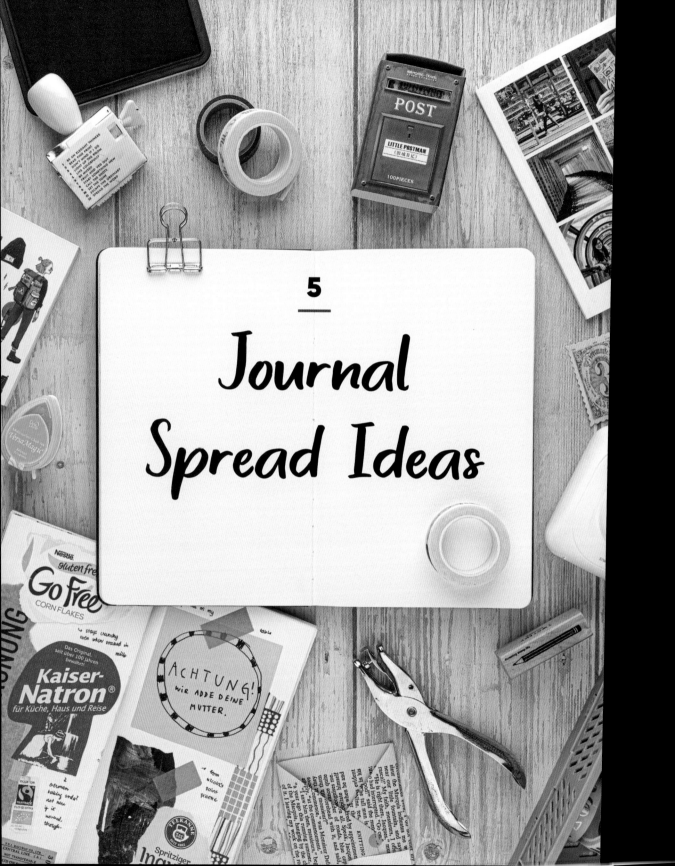

5

Journal Spread Ideas

The best part about travel journaling is the variety of ideas that can inspire fun projects to create. In this chapter, you'll get to know the anatomy of journal spreads, learn how to create themed pages sparked by your interests, and discover how you can incorporate hand lettering with journaling. You'll also learn how to combine different color schemes to build a cohesive palette for your journal pages.

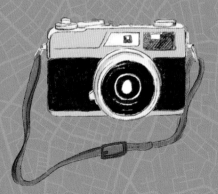

JOURNALING FORMATS

Documenting your travels can be intimidating, especially when you're faced with a blank page. Below are the main formats I follow when I journal. When I need a guide to start journaling, I turn to these formats for ideas and inspiration. Try them out!

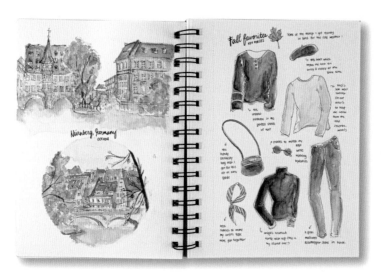

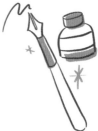

Art Heavy

An art-heavy journal spread features illustrated elements, using techniques such as drawing or lettering to create your journal page. Use a variety of tools such as pencil, ink, or paint to make the pages come to life.

This format allows your inner artist to shine through, whether you're hand lettering or fully illustrating or painting the journal spread.

Recommended Tools: Working in an art journal allows you to create using a variety of mediums, such as paint and markers. Art journal options include ones with watercolor paper or mixed media paper that stand up to wet mediums. These journals allow your creativity to flow on each page. A fountain pen filled with permanent ink or a fineliner pen are your best bets for drawing and doodling.

Text Heavy

If you have a handful of stories and essays to share about your travels, stick to a text-heavy format and let your words flow freely on paper. You can also use stationery to embellish the pages and add extra color.

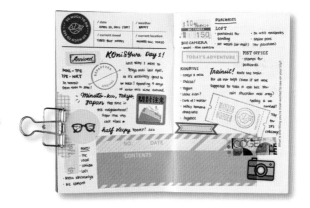

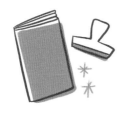

Recommended Tools: A pocket journal is a great way to log your immediate observations, as is a hardcover notebook that will be stable and spacious enough to fill up during your idle time in transit. Having a paper or binder clip is handy for marking pages you're working on.

Photo Heavy

Do you have a knack for capturing images and enjoy printing them out? Using a photo-heavy format showcases your visual creativity in the best way.

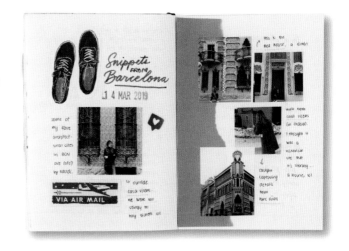

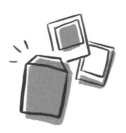

Recommended Tools: It's good to invest in a photo printer to print on the go, or you can have photos printed at photo shops while traveling. These pocket devices come in handy for your travel journaling needs.

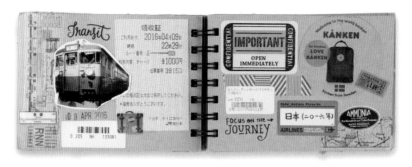

Collage Heavy

Channel your inner collage artist and use the ephemera you've collected to add character to your journal pages. For an added challenge, create color-coded spreads by using analogous colors or contrasting spreads by using complementary colors of ephemera.

Recommended Tools: Have a pair of pocket scissors and glue tape handy for creating collages on the go plus a folder or an envelope where you can temporarily store ephemera such as tickets and receipts.

The Ultimate Combination

If you can't choose one format, combine art, photos, collage, and text to build a balanced spread based on what you're documenting. Some things to remember for this layout style: Less is more, and it takes time to become comfortable with mixing elements on a page.

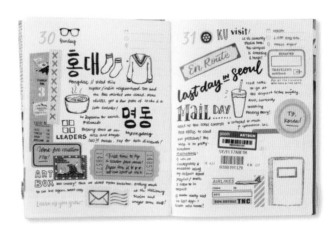

Recommended Tools: A nifty travel pouch or organizer for storing art and stationery supplies is essential, as you'll be drawing, writing, and using different techniques to create journal spreads.

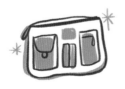

THEMED JOURNAL SPREADS

In the following pages, you'll find various themes to try, and you'll learn how to document them on your travel journal spreads.

Architecture

Architecture is one of the first things that catches my eye when I visit a new place. Something about seeing buildings and structures for the first time always piques my curiosity and makes me want to draw them.

You don't have to be a master architect or draw buildings perfectly to create travel journal spreads that feature interesting structures. I can't draw straight lines, so my architecture drawing style is looser and has a more free-form style. After all, what you see is what's reflected in your journal, and there are no rules.

I'm drawn to architecture because of how different it looks in every city based on different styles, such as Gothic, Baroque, Neoclassical, and more. Here are some ideas for adding architecture to your travel journal spreads.

(continued)

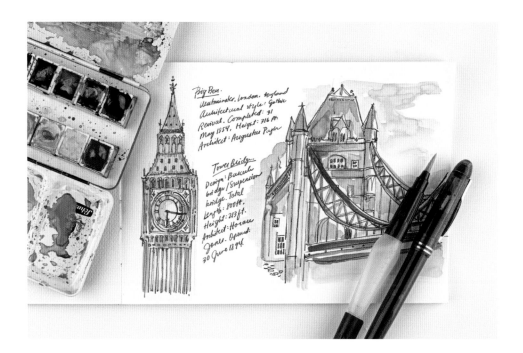

1 **Research and take pictures.** The first thing I do when I see unique architecture is identify the name of the building or structure and architectural style. This gives me a lot of ideas about how the structure was created and what style or styles it represents. If I'm on location, I'll take pictures of key details and the overall structure. If not, I'll look for reference photos online for inspiration.

2 **Focus and zoom in.** Immediately drawing what you see on your camera roll may be tempting, but I urge you to take a second look. What's the first thing you notice? Which details are you most attracted to? Focusing your attention like this is one of the key factors in drawing architecture. You don't have to draw the whole building; capturing certain elements helps tell the story without having to draw the entire structure.

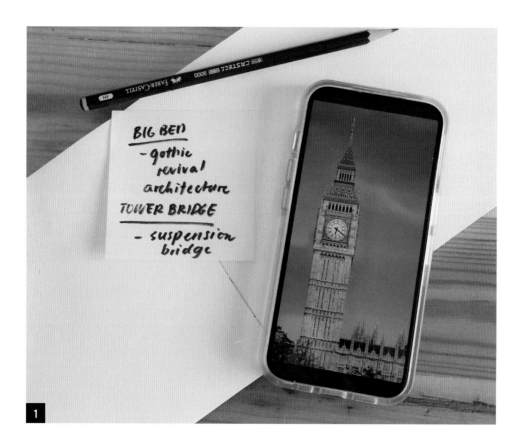

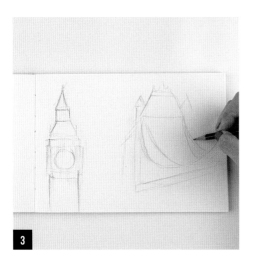

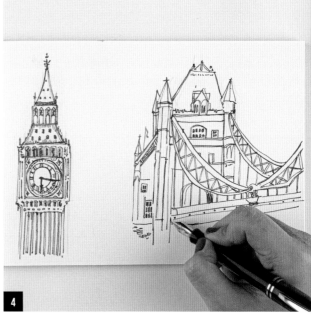

3   **Start with a loose sketch.** I start by creating shapes when drawing architecture, such as triangles, circles, squares, and rectangles. Use a hard lead pencil (which produces lighter lines) to sketch.

   To draw London's Big Ben, I focused on the major shapes and drew a rectangle for the tower, a triangle for the spire, and a circle for the clock. It doesn't have to be perfect, but what I like to do when sketching is have an overall guide on what I'm working with and where I could add further details into the artwork.

4   **Add the details.** Use a permanent fineliner pen or fountain pen filled with waterproof ink to outline and draw the structures. They say the devil's in the details, but I say choose the details you want to emphasize. Those can be a windowpane design, a clock atop a building, or the street lamps surrounding a city. You can leave the sketch as is or continue to the next step and add color.

(continued)

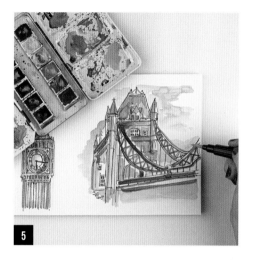

5   **Add color.** Color provides depth to your illustrations. For these subjects, I chose colors that were close to the original subject—blues for the sky and an ochre color for Big Ben and the Tower Bridge. I try to stay accurate with the subject I'm painting as it helps establish what the artwork is about.

One tip for painting is that in order to get a more saturated color, make sure you're using more pigment than water and wipe the excess water out so that it becomes more vibrant on paper.

6   **Write captions.** When I devote the majority of my journal pages to architectural drawings, usually the text comes last. This is when I can wrap up the journal pages and tell the story effectively through a short phrase or summary of my thoughts.

Journaling about architecture offers several options. These prompts will get you started.

- A landscape or a cityscape from your trip
- A page full of interesting windows, doors, or buildings from a city you've visited
- A favorite historical structure and its architectural origins (the Eiffel Tower in Paris, for example)

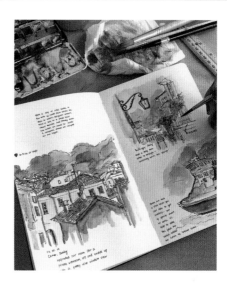

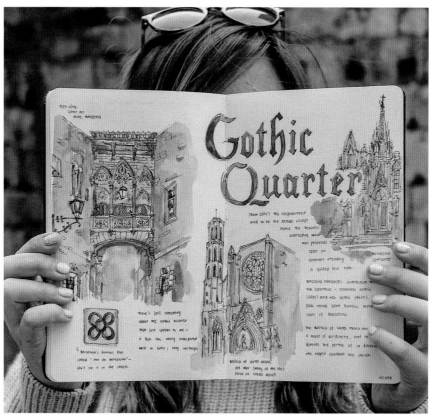

Food, Restaurants, and Cafés

Documenting your food adventures is a great way to create interesting and colorful pages for your travel journal. So much can be discovered through what we eat and drink in every city or country, including street food and local market finds.

Food is a fun topic to journal about. You can draw or paint what you've eaten, print photos to add to your journal pages, or collect food packaging to use as ephemera. Incorporating mixed media is also a great option, as it gives your pages more variety. Here I use markers as the main medium.

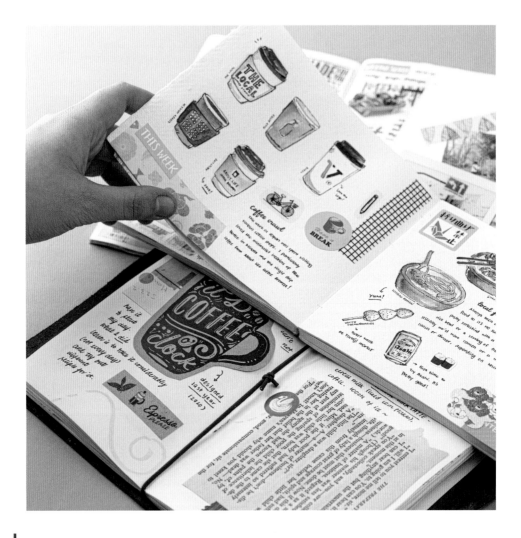

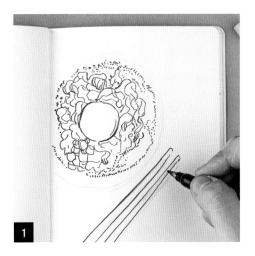

1. **Pencil in a sketch.** After you sketch, go over the lines with a permanent ink fineliner or brush pen. Adding an outline helps make it easier to color the image with markers or whatever medium you want to use. When drawing food, I try to capture key elements about the subject. Here, I drew a beef bowl and made sure I included a bowl, rice, beef, and an egg yolk to highlight the dish.

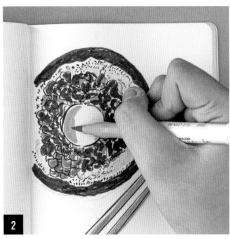

2. **Add color with markers.** Adding color to drawings of food with watercolor or markers highlights the different textures and is a wonderful creative exercise. I recommend sticking to the actual colors. For example, using a bright yellow for an egg yolk makes it look more appetizing and realistic. Also, leave some of the white of the page showing as highlights.

(continued)

Drawings add a beautiful and unique touch to a page, but you don't need advanced skills to add sketches to your journal pages. A quick outline of a coffee cup or a suggestion of something is enough.

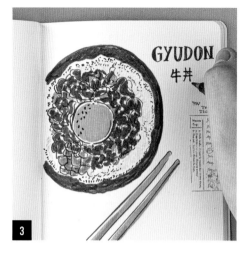

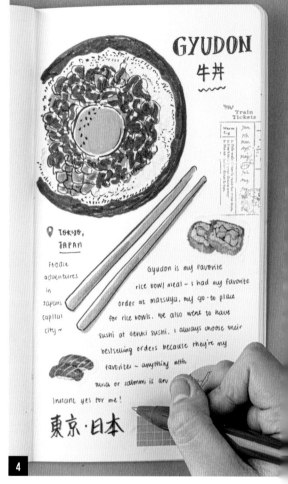

3 **Create a hand-lettered header to label your drawing.** I added Japanese characters and a printed serif font to spell *gyudon* (which translates to "Japanese beef and rice bowl") to add a bit of boldness to the page.

4 **Journal about the food.** Did you recently try this new dish you've drawn, or is this an all-time favorite when you're traveling? I find that art and text go hand in hand when telling a story through a journal.

5 **Add more interest to the page.** Use stickers, stamps, or ephemera. I added stickers, some washi tape, and a stamped train ticket.

Lettering Ideas

:::

As with drawing, your lettering doesn't have to be perfect—just have fun with it. Calligraphy books, magazines, shop and street signs, and packaging are great lettering inspiration. Adding elements such as small, simple drawings (such as the pizza slice and the fork and spoon) are easy ways to make headers and titles more noticeable. Surrounding words with banners and scrolls can also draw attention to lettering.

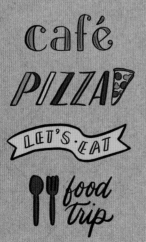

Let these prompts spark ideas for documenting your food adventures in your journal.

- Coffee shop log
- A trip to the grocery store or open-air market
- Favorite food discoveries
- Recipes
- Food history, culture, and traditions
- Food tours
- Bars and pubs
- Local food favorites

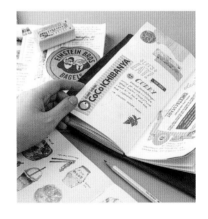

Trip Highlights

Recording your trip highlights helps condense the information in an efficient way. If you like keeping words to a minimum and prefer a more visual approach to travel journaling, this format will suit your style.

I recommend taking notes during your trip so you can plot out some features to add to the pages later. This helps you synthesize the information better and allows you to finalize key parts of your trip that are worth drawing attention to.

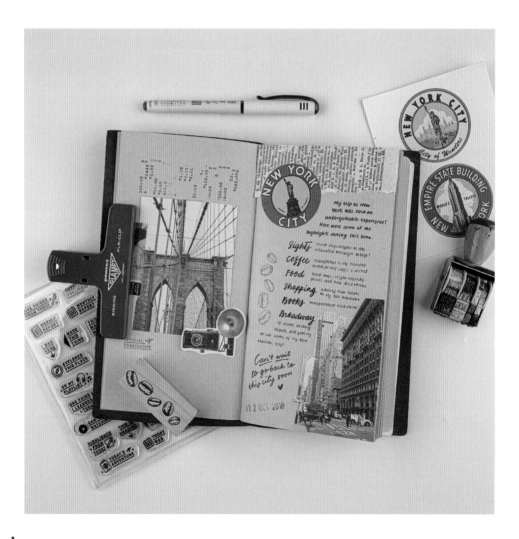

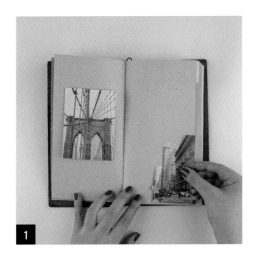

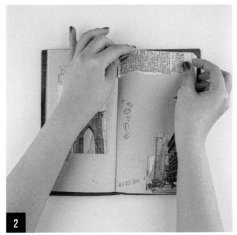

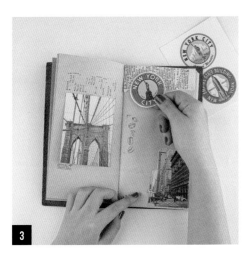

1 **Add your main subjects.** Determine the focal images you want to use for the spread. I chose some of my photos from a trip to New York and added these first because they establish the overall layout of my travel journal spread. This also helped me figure out the spacing I needed for text and other elements.

2 **Include stationery elements.** Add supplementary elements such as paper strips, ephemera, and stamps to bring dimension and character to the pages. I used a kraft journal for this project, so I made sure to incorporate elements that provided contrast, such as white paper strips and gray ink for the stamps.

3 **Enhance the pages with more elements.** Add more small elements, such as stickers and bits of ephemera that make the layout look more put together. Think about where you'll add text (I saved room on the right-hand page) and leave enough space to write. When including stationery, I always add pieces gradually and vary the shapes to make the pages look more interesting. The round NYC sticker, for example, creates a nice contrast with the torn paper edges.

(continued)

4 Write the text.

The final element of this page is the handwritten text, and the style is up to you. I typically create a "listicle" where I detail highlights and what I thought about them. You can also summarize your thoughts in a few paragraphs or phrases or include a short anecdote.

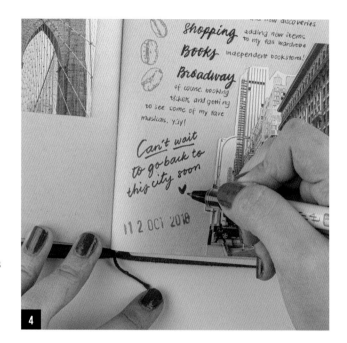

You can capture your trip highlights in many ways; here are a few more ideas.

- The top five highlights of your trip
- Fun facts about a city
- Draw snippets of your trip with one drawing a day

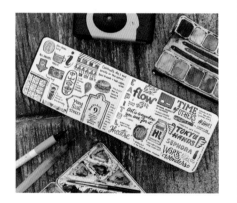

Museums and Galleries

I visit museums and galleries everywhere I travel, and I make sure to document these art-filled places when I'm in a new city. This serves as an official account of my trip and allows me to exercise curiosity and gain new knowledge about art in general.

Apart from journaling about your museum experiences, doing a deep dive on specific works of art, artists, art movements, and key information about the exhibitions is another way to expand your understanding about the topic. Start journaling about museums and galleries with these easy steps.

(continued)

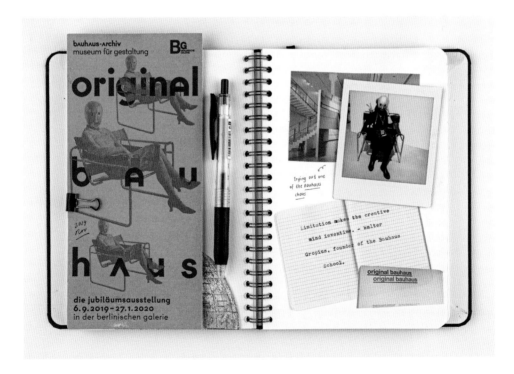

1. **Gather your museum-related ephemera.** This can include gallery maps, tickets, souvenir packaging, and photos. Keep them close by because they'll be your core pieces for this journal spread. I saved a piece of the exhibition map and used some photos that I cut up.

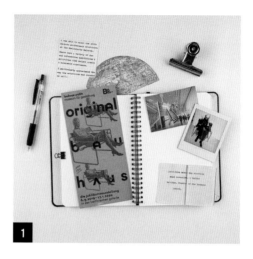

2. **Compose a layout based on your ephemera.** Position the pieces in different iterations to see which ones fit best, taking into consideration the size of the spread, the elements you'll include, and the amount of text you'll write. I clipped the map to the left-hand page, added some text, and used the right-hand page for photos and cutouts.

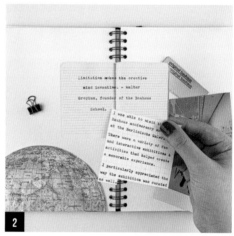

3. **Adhere pieces to the pages.** Once you're happy with the overall composition, adhere the elements one at a time to their designated places. I recommend using glue tape (see page 32) so the paper doesn't wrinkle. I tend to combine a handful of different types of ephemera to create my museum-themed journal page, so I like doing this part last. The remaining spaces will be allotted for text to round out the overall spread.

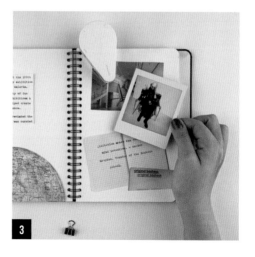

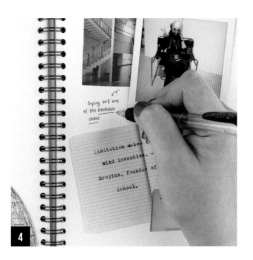

4 **Get creative with writing.** Write about the museum's history, add a quote from an artist, or do research on an art movement and how it juxtaposes with your journal spread. I typed out some of my journaling on scrap paper using a typewriter to add to the vintage feel I wanted on these pages. I included an overview of the exhibition and a notable quote from one of the architects involved, which is about the Bauhaus school and art movement.

Here are a few more ideas to try when documenting your trips to museums and galleries.

- Fill a journal page with museum entrance tickets.
- Feature your favorite artworks from a gallery trip.
- Create a museums bucket list for your next adventures.

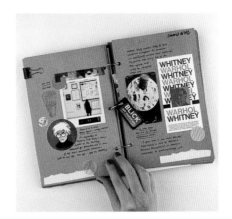

Documenting Adventures Close to Home

Having a journal on hand to document your life is always a good idea, whether you're going on an extended road trip or a weekend adventure. Travel journaling isn't always about trips to exotic locales; capturing adventures close to home can be just as meaningful and satisfying.

My friends and I would spend weekends during the summer driving a few hours from the city to try a new restaurant, stay at a new resort, or have some quiet time at the beach. This has always been my favorite way to de-stress and get away from the hustle and bustle of city life, even for a few days. I always make sure to have a small journal with me to document the little things that make these quick adventures memorable.

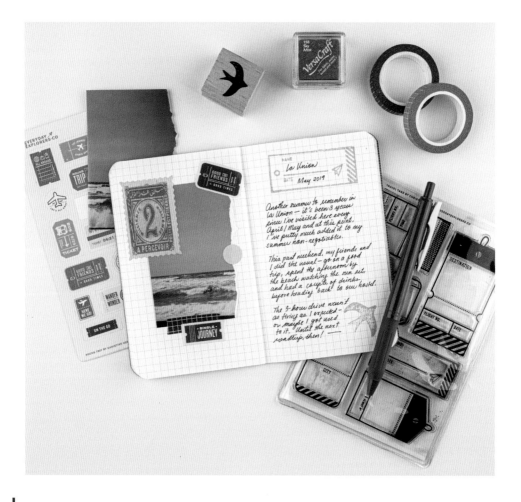

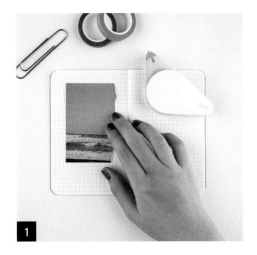

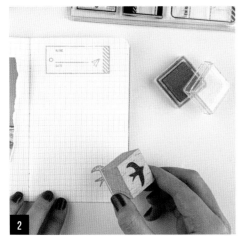

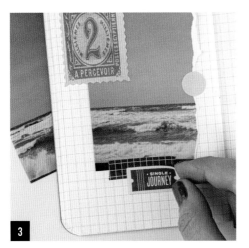

1 **Gather and add photos.** One way to spice up a photo is to tear one side of the image to create character and personality. For this spread I used a photo of the sea, which I captured using my film camera. I ripped the right-hand side to mimic the waves.

2 **Get stamping.** Take note of dominant colors where you are, whether that's by the sea or on a hiking trip. Use the colors as your main theme and incorporate stationery elements to suit the pages. I stamped some images in blue ink to capture the essence of the sea photo and to create the calm energy that reminds me of water.

3 **Embellish the pages.** When the spread is almost complete, add a few extra touches to fully capture the overall theme and help it come together. I added a dot sticker to contrast the shapes on the journal pages. A little goes a long way.

(continued)

4 Keep your writing short and sweet.
Writing about adventures close to home allows me to keep my writing to the point. I make sure to write something personal that will help me remember that specific moment in time, whether it's a short anecdote or a brief paragraph about memorable parts of the weekend.

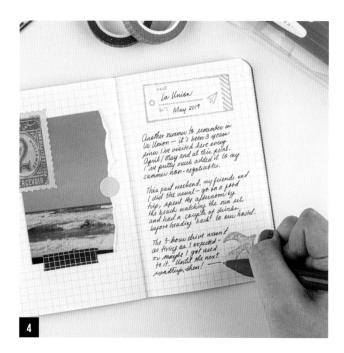

Documenting your adventures allows you to get creative and notice the little things that transpire during your vacations and downtime. Here are a few more prompts you can try.

- A memorable road trip
- A favorite weekend spot
- An adventure with nature at the mountains or the beach

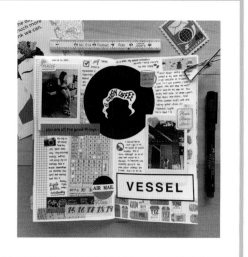

HAND LETTERING

Hand lettering is the art of drawing letters and is one way to incorporate original art into your travel journals—the art of the written word, that is. I've been doing lettering for many years now, and it's something I always try to incorporate with other creative projects I do, travel journaling included.

Here are some common types of fonts that can be used for hand lettering:

- **Serif:** a font style that has short lines at the ends of letter strokes and evokes a classic and traditional style
- **Sans serif:** a font without the serifs and evokes a modern and youthful style
- **Script:** a font that flows much like our own handwriting and evokes an elegant style

You may have encountered brush lettering, by definition a lettering style that uses a brush pen to create fluid strokes that vary in thickness to create a distinct style. This is closely related to script fonts and is a fun way to enhance your cursive handwriting.

You can create lettering using any writing or drawing tool. Hand lettering can enhance your travel journal pages by adding more character and a personal touch to your pages.

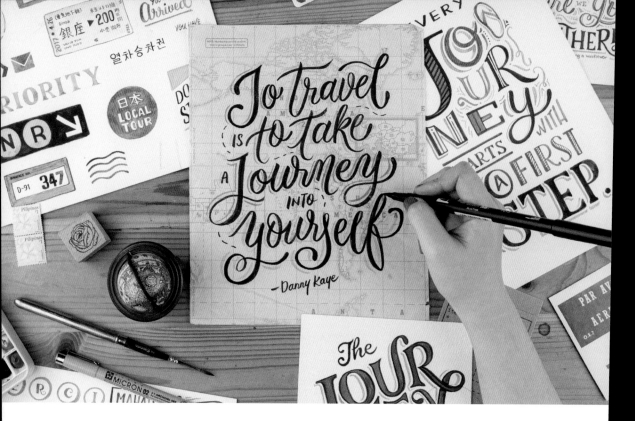

A font is a set of letters in a specific color or size. Brush lettering, on the other hand, is a type of font that features mostly script style lettering and uses a brush pen to achieve that technique.

Here are some ideas for things to letter.

- Names of countries or cities
- A quote or phrase you found inspiring during your trip
- Titles or headings of your journal spreads

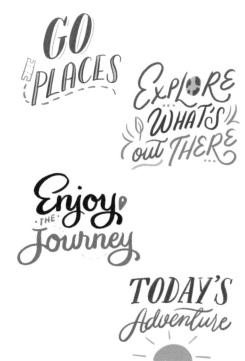

<table>
<tr><td>**Lesson**</td><td># HAND LETTERING IN YOUR JOURNAL</td></tr>
</table>

In this example, the word *PARIS* becomes the focus of the journal spread, with words surrounding the journal layout.

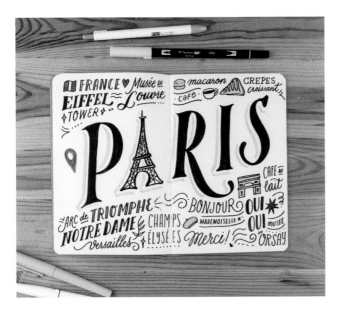

MATERIALS

- Pencil

- Marker-friendly journal (one with paper that's at least 100gsm)

- Brush pen or fineliner pen (I used a 2-in-1 brush pen and felt-tip pen in black, beige, and red)

1   Pencil in the main word on the spread. Start by opening your journal spread and dividing the letters into the two pages. I'm using a serif font style here that's a bit stylized; I made it more condensed so it looks tall. To divide it accordingly, I've drawn the word *PARIS* in the center, placing the letters *P* and *A* on the left page and *R*, *I*, and *S* on the right page. I made the letter *A* more illustrative by turning it into the Eiffel Tower because both have the same basic form. I created a simple design for the tower, but by including the iconic structural elements, the shape is immediately recognizable.

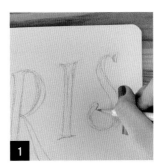

(continued)

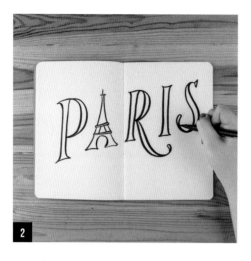

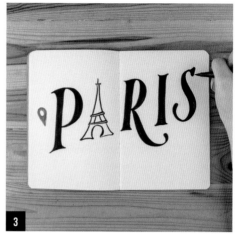

2   Using a brush pen or fineliner pen, outline the letters. When you're working with brush pens, take note that the tip is relatively larger, and it's easier to fill in letters by maximizing the different pressures. Adding more pressure on your brush pen will make it more of a paintbrush, while adding less pressure or using a light grip will make it more of a felt-tip pen for outlines and details.

3   Once everything is outlined, fill in the letterforms for a bolder effect. I added a geolocation icon with red pen.

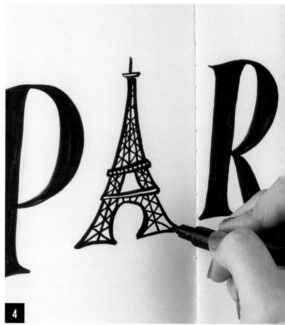

4   Add more lines to the Eiffel Tower to create the familiar lattice pattern.

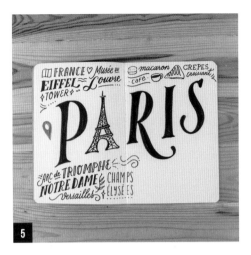

5

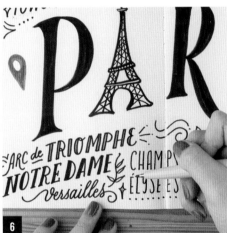

6

5 Because the area around the word is completely empty, I filled it up with more words that reminded me of my trip to Paris, including places I visited (the Louvre and Arc de Triomphe) and some favorite foods I tried (macarons and crepes). Think of something similar as a prompt for your spread: What did you love about a certain city or country you visited?

6 Loosely sketch the words to allot space for each one or go freestyle. Make sure there is adequate space between the focal word and the surrounding words. Try different lettering styles and add small doodles between the words to make the pages stand out more.

For the lettering styles in these pages, I jazzed up my handwriting by making letters bolder, using different fonts for a specific word, and adding little embellishments such as waves and rays as fillers for the empty spaces.

I made sure to cover up the pages with lettering styles that would not overpower the focus, which is the word *PARIS*. These elements complement the journal spread.

(continued)

7   With a lighter colored pen, add lines around your main word to create depth. This also distinguishes it more from the surrounding art. The shadows are directed to the left with the upper-right side being the light source. I am using a neutral-colored brush pen here to add a little distinction from the rest of the elements on the page. It's subtle, but it cuts across and helps create more space between the focus and the rest of the lettered elements on the spread.

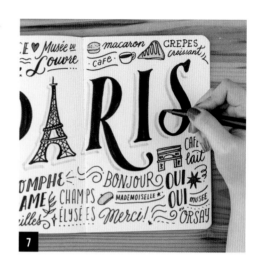

Here are some common words or phrases you can use for your travel journal pages.

- Let's go places
- Today's adventure
- Enjoy the journey
- En route
- Bonjour / Ciao / Hola!

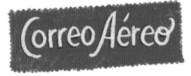

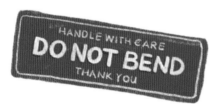

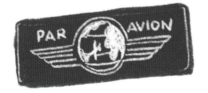

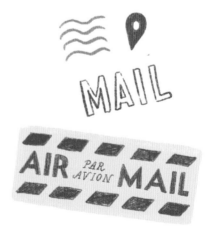

USING COLOR PALETTES TO TELL A STORY

Having an established color scheme for a journal spread helps guide the viewer's eye around the page and sets the mood, whether you're incorporating color with illustrations, premade elements, or both.

When traveling, I observe the various colors that represent each destination I visit, such as a country's flag or the season. Using a color palette to guide your journaling process is a great way to exercise your creativity and differentiate your pages. Working with a limited palette also makes journaling easier, especially if you don't have access to all your materials while traveling.

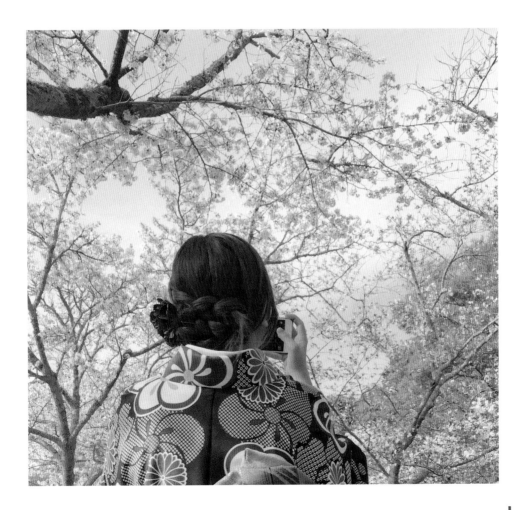

Here are some examples of color palettes inspired by cities and their seasons.

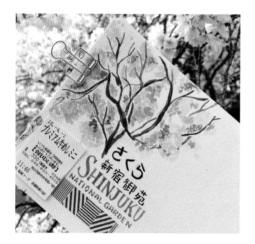

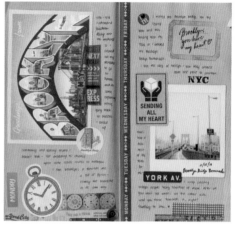

Spring in Tokyo

I frequently visit Tokyo during the springtime, so it's no surprise that cherry blossoms instantly establish the main color for my paintings and journal pages. Spring is a season when flowers bloom and is a stark contrast from the cold and white wintertime, so the predominant colors I use are mostly pink, green (for nature), and brights. I often visit Shinjuku Gyoen National Garden in Tokyo to people-watch and paint on location, and this inspired me to create a cherry blossom painting and pink and green journal pages.

Autumn in New York

With its warm brown hues, autumn is my favorite season. I frequently travel from September through November, so capturing the season has been a staple in my journaling process. During my time in New York, I grew fond of Brooklyn and would spend weekends exploring the borough and discovering new sights and coffee shops. This inspired my travel journals. I opted for a kraft journal and used autumn-themed stationery elements to create my journal spreads.

How to Select Color Palettes

- **Consider the weather and time of year where you're going.** Colors vary by season, making this an easy identifier for documenting your travels. Even daily changes such as sunny weather or a downpour can influence your creative vision. It pays to take note of these details when traveling. The soft pastel colors I captured in my photo of springtime in Japan are reflected in the hues I selected for this journal page: pink, aqua, and lavender.

- **Use your favorite colors as a starting point.** Knowing which shades you gravitate toward helps establish the color family you'll incorporate into your journal pages. I favor yellows, greens, and browns, and most of my journal spreads have a similar color scheme. This spread capturing a trip to New York incorporates my preferred colors and gives the pages a cozy feel with a kraft-colored clothing tag, patterned washi tape, and stickers in fall hues; autumnal leaf designs and motifs; and sepia-colored lettering.

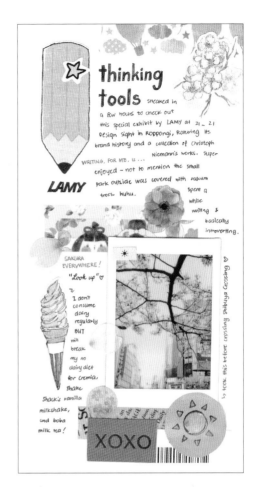

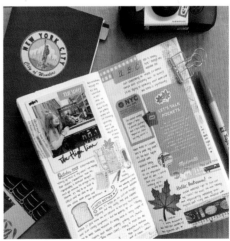

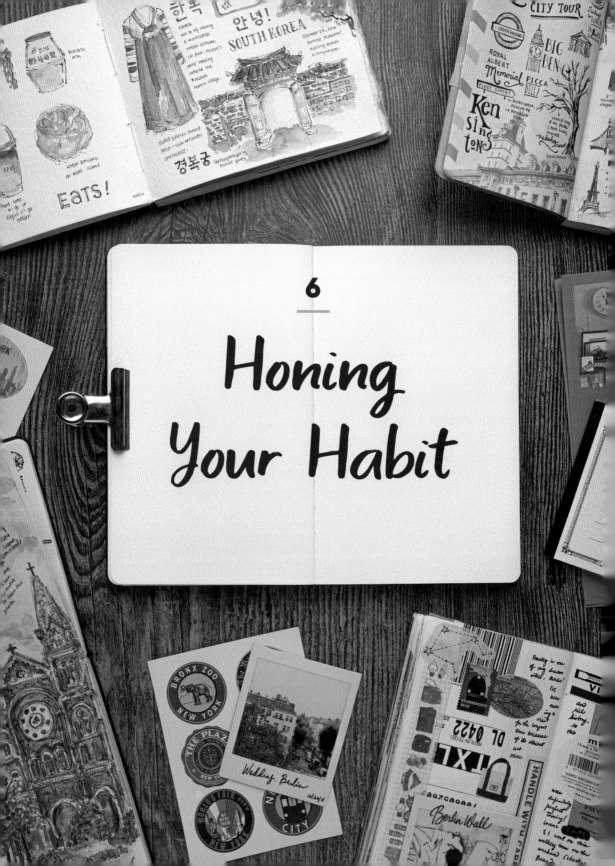

6

Honing
Your Habit

In this chapter you'll find insights and tips on how to store your journals, take photos to share on social media, and hone your ongoing travel journaling habit as you continue to embark on new adventures.

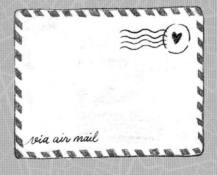

FINDING YOUR JOURNALING STYLE

The best part of travel journaling is that there are no rules. Journaling is simply a matter of figuring out what you love about travel and putting those ideas in a journal as an account of your adventures. I'll share some ways you can find and develop your unique journaling style.

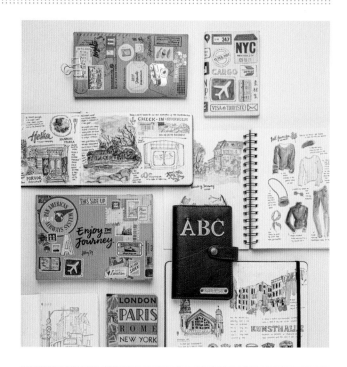

Explore the Possibilities

I can't tell you how many different journals I own—they vary in size, paper type, and brand. No two journal spreads are the same because I like exploring different ways to document.

The world is your oyster—or in this case, your journal is your oyster! Explore all the ways you can journal (I've shared lots of ideas in this book) and don't be afraid to experiment. Try different journal sizes and get inspired by a variety of prompts.

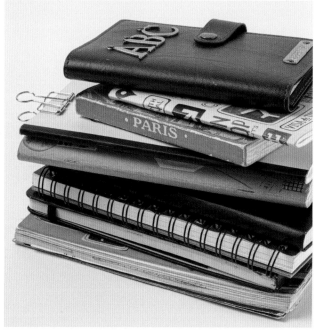

Embrace Your Creative Process

Travel journaling has no end goal. But if you're keen on improving certain skills such as drawing, collaging, or taking photos, keeping tabs on your progress is a way to develop your style. Embracing your creative process should be something worth noting, even more than progress itself. We have different approaches to our creative pursuits, and this is what makes us unique in telling stories from our own perspectives.

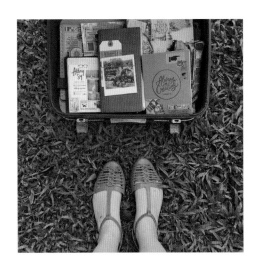

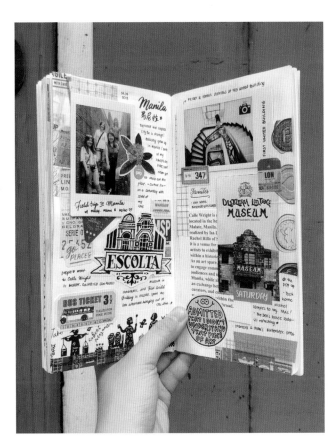

Keep Documenting (and Traveling)

A foolproof way of developing your journaling style is to keep documenting—and traveling! You never know what you'll encounter in a new city or country, and that may inspire your process in ways you can't imagine. Remember, developing a certain style shouldn't define the way you document; it should give you an opportunity to create something that is truly your own.

STAYING COMMITTED

Show Up Regularly

You don't have to journal every day, but showing up is always key. Whether it's once or twice in a trip or dedicating half an hour every day to journal, showing up can mean many things. But it's all about making it a part of your priority list.

Your preferred journaling time may be while in transit or after a trip has concluded. Are you most inspired to journal in the mornings, early afternoons, or evenings? Knowing these important factors will help you be more inspired to create and make time to create journal spreads.

Consider how much you want to accomplish in a journaling session. You can complete a page, two pages, or just half a page. Carving out time to journal and honing your habit are essential.

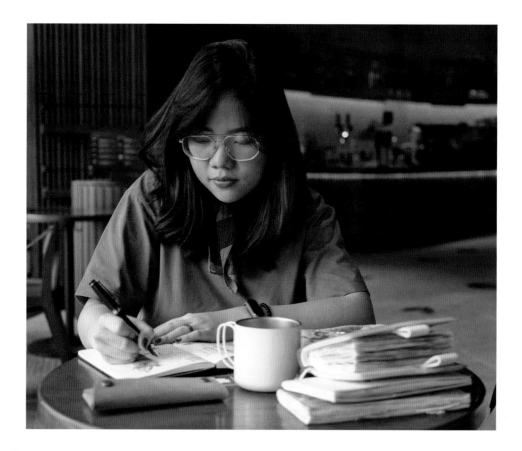

Choose a Medium That Suits You

Choose a medium that suits you now but also allows you to explore something different. This allows your journaling style to evolve and change over time. Change can be scary, but it also makes way for growth and more good things. Embrace it when it happens.

I had a fineliner pen with me at all times when I started travel journaling. As I continued to travel, I learned how to use watercolor for my journaling process. Eventually, I tried different mediums and techniques, using ephemera, collage, and mixed media for my travel journals. The best part is that I'm still finding new ways to create as I keep journaling.

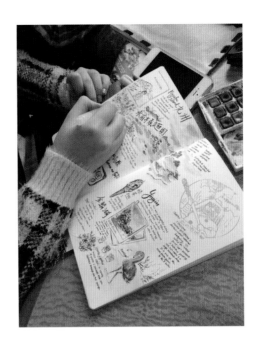

Take Time to Reflect

Sometimes we get so consumed with wanting to journal that we forget what we're journaling about. When you obsess over what the journal spread will look like rather than take time to look back on the memory itself, the process can become disillusioning.

Remember that travel journaling is a way for us to build a deeper relationship with travel and ourselves. How we see and capture moments reflects on what we create, so think about that when documenting in your journal.

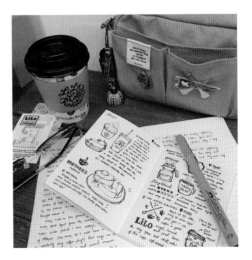

Make Journaling a Priority

Bring the same level of commitment to journaling that you bring to booking a ticket for your next trip. Make journaling a priority by bringing your travel art kit with you or take your pocket journal along wherever you go. You never know what you'll find when traveling.

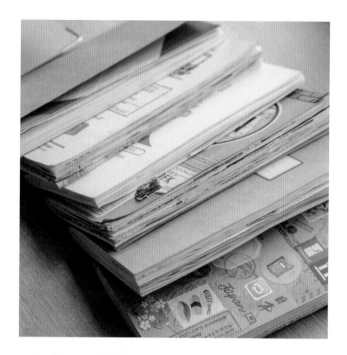

Explore and Travel More

What's travel journaling without travel? Keep honing your journaling habit by taking on more adventures, near and far. You'll be surprised by the wonderful adventures you have yet to embark on.

Consider joining journaling groups, hangouts, or even meetups. This can open your network to new friends and connections and could inspire you further on your travel journaling journey.

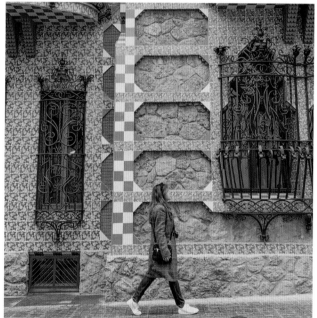

TIPS AND ADVICE TO LIVE BY

Invest in Quality Materials

In the seven years I've been travel journaling, I've learned that investing in good, archival materials is key to a better and more enjoyable journaling experience. I figured out what works best for me after trying new materials and different types of paints, pens, and supplies and learning more about what I use.

    With traveling comes the bonus of discovering new materials when you're in a foreign place, so capitalize on that by visiting art stores, bookstores, and stationery stores. You'll be delighted to see the variety of art materials and new tools you'll find.

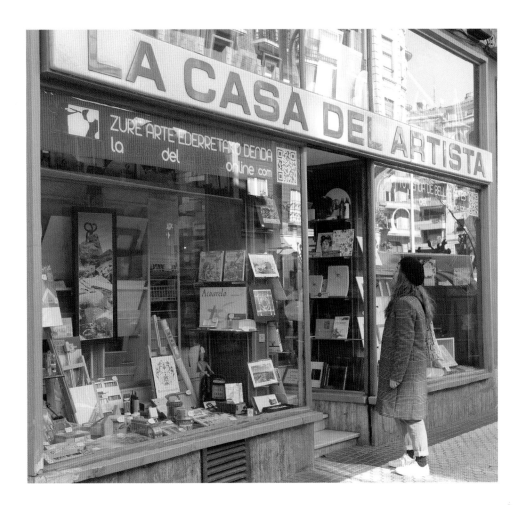

Consistency Is Key

By "consistency," I don't mean staying with the same journal size (that could work, though) or using the same tools; I mean being a consistent journaler. No matter what medium, theme, or tools you're using, as long as you keep journaling, you'll be done.

I've never been one who's stuck to a formula when it comes to journaling. I think the only regular thing I've done is use a specific journal size for collage journaling. Other than that, my preferences ebb and flow as I see fit and as I keep exploring new places.

Continue to Experiment

If I travel to the same location every few years, I don't document the same things or even use the same style. I've also never been a creature of habit, so trust me when I say it's okay not to record every single trip.

I do try to experiment all the time, thinking about what I can notice and document. Even the mundanity of people, places, and things can spark inspiration. A conversation with someone may inspire you to try a new style or capture new subjects. Anything is possible.

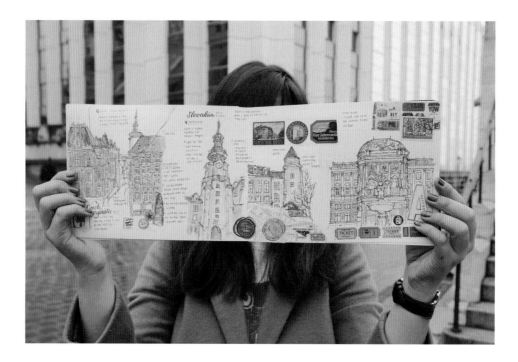

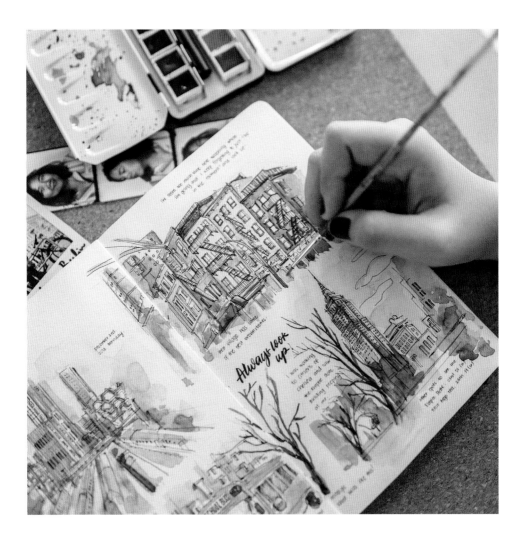

Play to Your Strengths

I don't see travel journaling as a competitive art form; there's no measure of good or bad when it comes to documenting. Journaling is a solo endeavor, and you can only judge how good or bad your own journal is. Honestly, though, there are no bad journals.

I advise you to play to your strengths and work your way from there. If you like to draw, use that to your advantage. If you enjoy the combination of drawing and writing like I do, maximize your skills and use them as a way to document. This allows you to find a comfortable area where you can use this style anytime you like while venturing into something new when the mood strikes.

Remember Why You Started

I'd like you to revisit two things: identifying your journaling purpose (see page 17) and your first travel journal, if you've made one. What inspired you to start documenting your adventures? And what keeps you going? What made you pick up this book?

I hope you discover your motivation for travel journaling. Once you do, remember it. You can always take breaks in the process. Pace yourself—this is your journaling journey, and you can choose what's best for you. Still, never forget why you started doing this and where it can take you. As Homer said, "The journey is the thing."

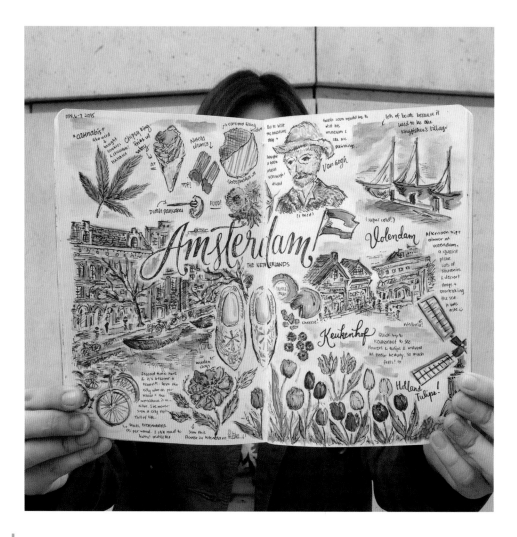

7

Guest Artists

Looking for more ideas and inspiration for your travel journal? In this chapter, I invited some of my friends and fellow artists to share their travel journal pages, favorite supplies, and go-to cities for travel journaling. Take a look at their wonderfully documented travels and adventures in their journal pages, which include techniques such as collage, illustration, and mixed media.

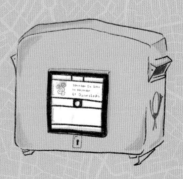

JANE LEE

Website: hellojanelee.com
Instagram: @janethecrazy
Location: Kuala Lumpur, Malaysia
Favorite art supply: A pen for writing; currently liking the Sarasa colored ink gel pen.

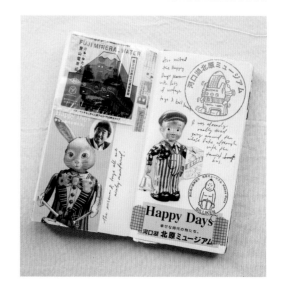

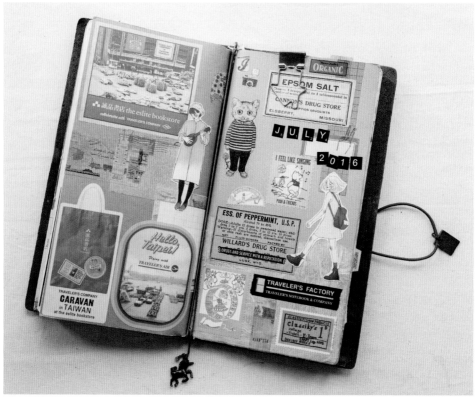

JULIA MOROTCHENKO

Instagram: @julia.s_journals
YouTube: Crafty Raccoon
Location: Visby, Sweden
Journaling style: Vintage

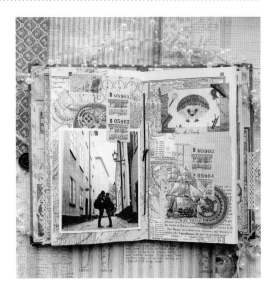

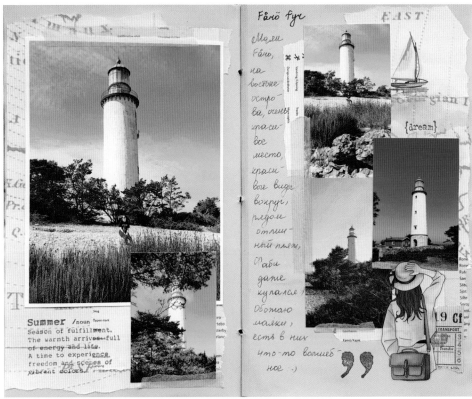

MELISSA TAN

Website: tangerine-studiosg.com
Instagram: @tangerine.studiosg
Location: Singapore
Favorite city or country: Berlin, Germany

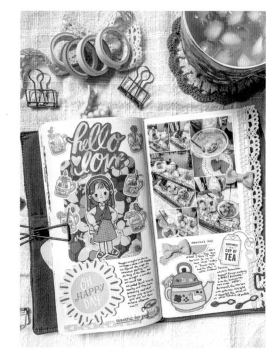

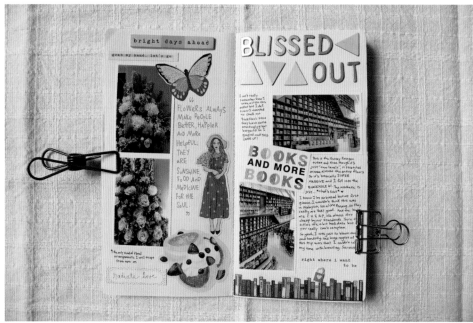

HELEN COLEBROOK

Website: journalwithpurpose.co.uk
Instagram: @journalwithpurpose
Location: United Kingdom
Journaling style: Decorative, often in a vintage style, with plenty of room for writing.

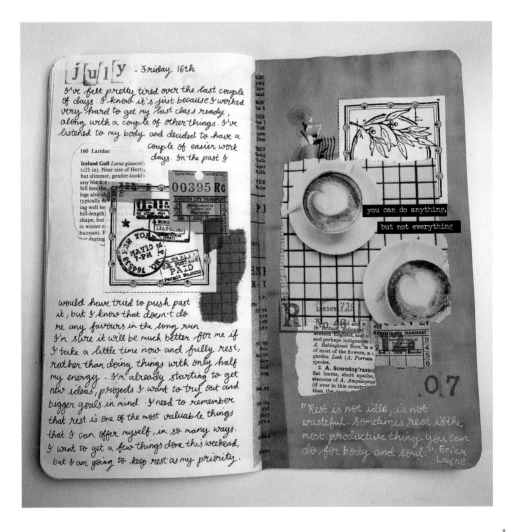

JOB AIRAM

Website: jobsjournal.org
Instagram, TikTok:
@jobsjournal
Twitch: jobsjournal
YouTube: Job's Journal
Location: Vancouver,
Canada
Favorite art supply:
Washi tape

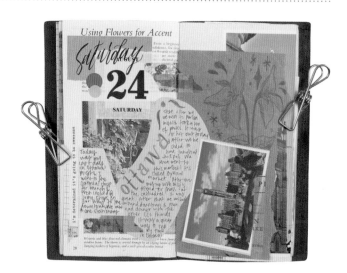

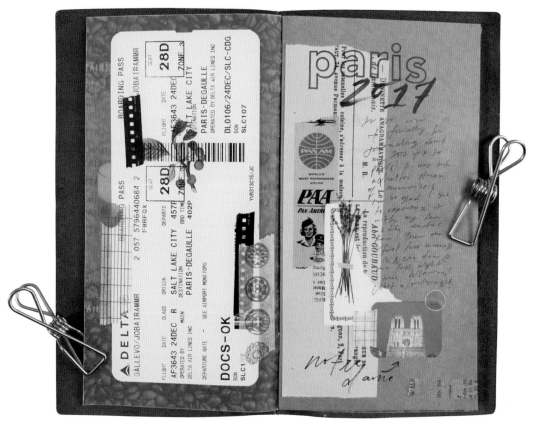

YULIA

Instagram: @yulia_pc
Location: Saitama, Japan
Favorite city or country: Japan—and now I live there!

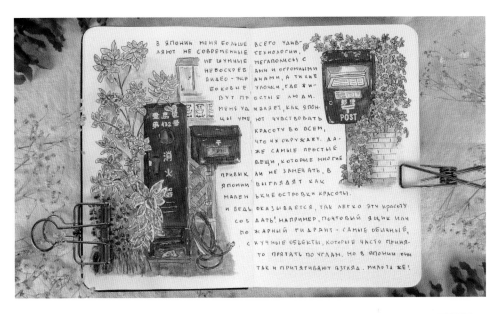

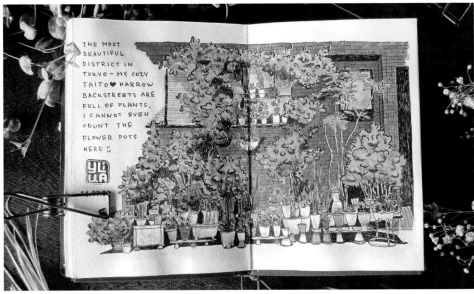

THE MOST BEAUTIFUL DISTRICT IN TOKYO — MY COZY TAITO♥ NARROW BACKSTREETS ARE FULL OF PLANTS, I CANNOT EVEN COUNT THE FLOWER POTS HERE ☺

CHRISTINE HERRIN

Website: everydayexplorers.co

Instagram: @christine.herrin, @everydayexplorersco

Location: Berkeley, California, USA

Favorite city or country: London—it's the perfect mix of history, art, design, and culture.

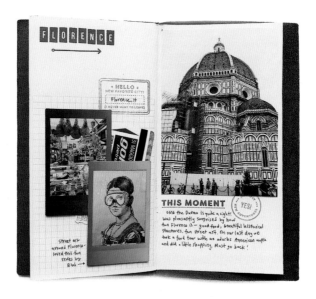

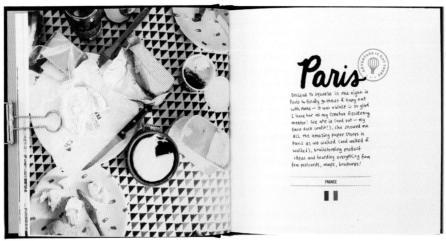

CHELSEA PARK

Website: thosewithwords.com
Instagram: @thosewithwords
Location: San Francisco, California, USA
Preferred journal size: A5 for planning, standard traveler's notebook for creative journaling.

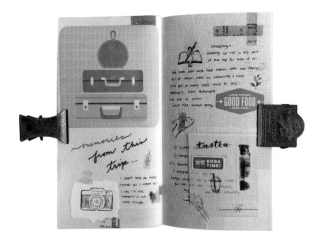

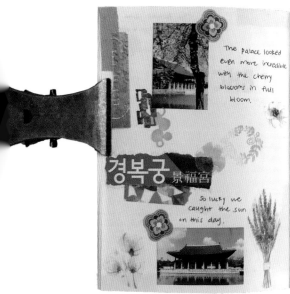

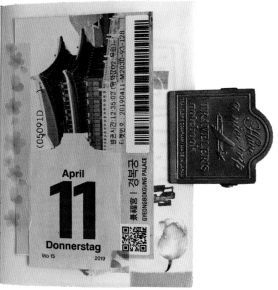

MITS N

Instagram: @mylifemits
YouTube: MyLifeMits
Location: Tokyo, Japan
Journaling style:
A mashup of everything
that she adores. There
are days of color and
days of calm, just like
daily life.

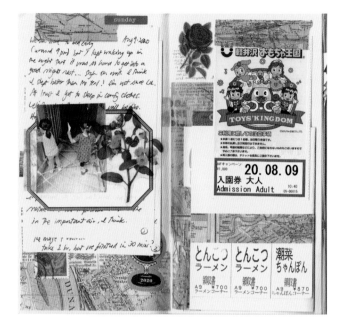

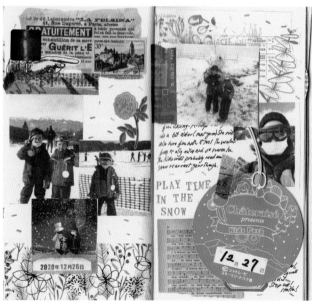

ERI SALCEDO

Instagram: @_sakuralala_
YouTube: Sakuralala
Location: Tokyo, Japan
Favorite art supply:
Stamps, washi tapes,
watercolor, midliner pen,
ephemera

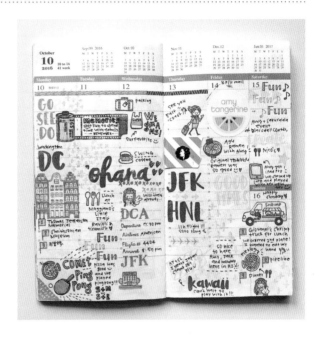

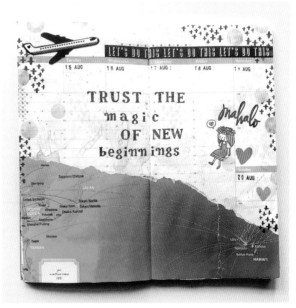

CAYLEE GREY

Instagram: @cayleegrey
Website: cayleegrey.com
Location: Bruchsal, Germany
Favorite city or country: Berlin, Germany. It feels like German Cape Town (South Africa), the perfect merging of my two homes. There's something raw and gritty about it, and the coffee shops are perfect for spending hours journaling.

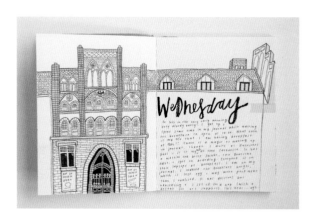

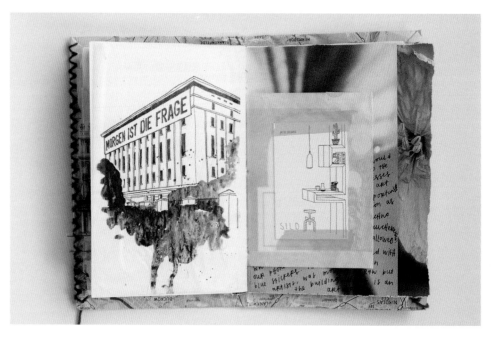

Resources

Collage Graphics

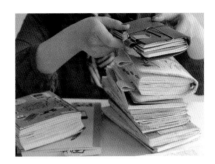

- **Graphics Fairy:** graphicsfairy.com
- **Nearness Project:** nearnessproject.com
- **Rookie Magazine:** rookiemag.com

Acknowledgments

Writing this book was such an adventure. Being able to revisit my travels through the pages of my journals and develop a deeper relationship with documenting was such a treat.

I'd like to thank my editor, Jeannine, for pitching this idea to me, helping me create a book from something that is so close to my heart, and being so helpful and supportive every step of the way. A few years ago I wrote "write a book about travel journaling" as one of my goals, and now it's finally real.

Thank you to Quarto for allowing me to share my love for travel journaling through the publication of this book. I am always grateful to the team behind my books for helping make this possible, from *Hand Lettering A to Z* to now.

Thank you to my photographer and friend, Cherisse, for all the beautiful photos and for helping me organize them to fit each and every page. Thank you, Stacey, for all the additional help in putting this book together!

My work sprints were made possible thanks to my trusty analog timer and virtual work sessions with the Always Be Creating Art Club. The Beatles songs were on loop every time I would write or edit, and that helped me ease into the writing process.

I'm extending my thanks to everyone who has helped pave the way for this new book to happen—people I've worked with in the past, readers who have bought and supported my previous books, and my community for all the support.

Lastly, to my friends and family, thank you for all the moral support!

About the Author

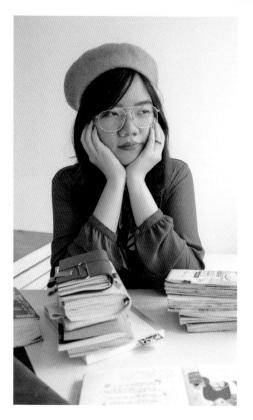

Abbey Sy is an artist and author whose creative career includes writing and illustrating books on hand lettering, journaling, and living a creative life.

With a love for art and travel, Abbey has dedicated her life to exploring new places, documenting them in her journals, and building a community that provides ideas and inspiration for your creative journey.

This is Abbey's seventh book. Her other books are *The ABCs of Hand Lettering*, *The ABCs of Journaling*, and *Always Be Creating: A Field Guide to Living a Creative Life*. Her Quarto titles are *Hand Lettering A to Z*, *The Complete Photo Guide to Hand Lettering and Calligraphy*, and *Hand Lettering A to Z Workbook*. She lives in Berlin, Germany.

Website: abbeysy.com
Instagram: @abbeysy, @shopabbeysy, @alwaysbecreating.art
YouTube: youtube.com/abbeysy
Patreon: patreon.com/abbeysy

Index